D0560543

DISCARD

This House On Fire

This House On Fire

The Story of the Blues

by Craig Awmiller

The African-American Experience

Franklin Watts
A Division of Grolier Publishing
New York/London/Hong Kong/Sydney
Danbury, Connecticut

Acknowledgments

Sincere acknowledgment and thanks must be extended to the blues scholars Albert Murray, Sam Charters, Alan Lomax, Sandra Lieb, Charles Sawyer, Charles Wolf, Kip Lornell, Robert Santelli, William Barlow, Robert Palmer, John Chilton, James Lincoln Collier, Paul Oliver, Max Harrison, William Bolcom, Bob Brunning, and Peter Guralnick, without whom a book of this kind would not have been possible.

*This book is dedicated to James Alan McPherson,
who first told me about the blues, and to Mose Vinson,
who first showed me how to play them.*

Frontispiece: *Howlin' Wolf (1910–76) in 1971*

Photographs copyright ©: Peter Amft: frontispiece, pp. 132, 139; The New York Historical Society, New York City: p. 14; Archive Photos: p. 19; The Bettmann Archive: pp. 23, 57; Cammarata Archives: pp. 29, 87 (both Jas Obrecht); Frank Driggs Collection: pp. 38, 93, 124 (all Joe Alper), 33, 48, 73, 115, 128; Mimosa Record Productions: p. 42; Michael Ochs Archives: pp. 52, 82, 135; London Features International (USA) Ltd.: pp. 102, 109, 143 (Joe Hughes); Jim Marshall: p. 119.

Library of Congress Cataloging-in-Publication Data

Awmiller, Craig.
    This house on fire: the story of the blues / by Craig Awmiller.
        p.   cm.—(The African-American experience)
    Includes bibliographical references and index.
    Summary: Gives a history of blues music from its origins in the 1800s to the present day, with discussions of its African roots and its influence on other music.
    ISBN 0-531-11253-5 (lib bdg.)—ISBN 0-531-15797-0 (pbk.)
    1. Blues (Music)—History and criticism—Juvenile literature. [1. Blues (Music)]
I. Title.   II. Series.
ML3521.A96 1996
781.643'09—dc20   96-10290
                                                                                        CIP
                                                                                    AC MN

Contents

Introduction

What images come to mind when you think about the music called "the blues"?

You might picture Dan Aykroyd and John Belushi doing their "Jake and Elwood" act in *The Blues Brothers*, hopping around onstage wearing thin ties, sunglasses, and porkpie hats. Or you might imagine a sweating black man, bending notes on an electric guitar in a smoky ghetto bar, wailing that his baby has done him wrong. Or maybe a few old names float by. Funny names, such as "Blind Lemon," "Leadbelly," and "Son House"—and with these names, perhaps some of the haunting music they left behind, music almost always poorly recorded, played on simple, even crude instruments.

Hollywood actors. Someone crying about lost love. Strange names. Each of these images are familiar stereotypes, myths that tell little about the blues. The true story of the blues is infinitely more rich, more complex, and more meaningful than these fleeting images. The true story of the blues is not one of movie stars, myths, and names without faces. It is instead one of courage and artistry, of tenacity and genius, as created by real men and women in a real world. By studying the lives of these African-American men and women we can get a little closer to the truth about the blues.

7

A short book like this one can never do the blues justice. The subject is just too big. There are just too many individuals who deserve mention, too many styles to explore, and too many social, economic, and psychological factors that must be accounted for in order to gain a full understanding of this music. Even among blues historians there are varying opinions on who did what, when, and why, and what it all meant. So the most I can give here is an introduction. With every name I mention, there's a half dozen I've left out.

There's another reason, though, why this book—and probably *any* book on the blues—will be incomplete. The blues—especially in its early years, with its beginnings in rural, folk, and oral traditions—simply has no hard-and-fast recorded history. For each blues master we know of, for each Bessie Smith, Robert Johnson, and Muddy Waters, it is possible that there is another unknown, unrecorded master whose voice will never be heard.

It is impossible to say how many names and how much music have been lost this way, lost to the fact that almost every "serious" student of music in those early days—that is, the beginning of the twentieth century—thought the blues were an inferior form of "race" music, and so did not merit close study. And, sadly, as the years progressed, commercial and folkloric documentation of this music did not always improve. For example, the final recordings of Blind Willie McTell, a blues virtuoso from Georgia, were saved from destruction at the last moment when the owner of a house that was being demolished took a final look through his attic and accidently came across McTell's long-lost tapes. Thanks to this lucky turn of events, a blues classic was saved. But who knows how many other beginning, middle, and final sessions of how many other artists have been lost.

So, that's my apology and warning. If you're looking for stereotypes, myths, or an exhaustive treatment of the blues, look elsewhere because you won't find them here. But if you're looking for a real introduction, some idea as to why this music is so powerful and why it influences artists as diverse as Bruce Springsteen, Wynton Marsalis, and Arrested Development, then read on. The blues, as you will find out, are more than simply a kind of music: they are a way of thinking, a way of looking at the world, a hard-won philosophy. And even better than simply learning about this blues outlook from a book, go on from here and find the music at a record store, a public library, or a friend's house, and listen. In the notes and words crackling from those recordings, in the sighs and whoops and howls of the musicians preserved there, you'll hear the true story of the blues—a story that, if you understand it, will change you.

That's what it does to everyone.

Always has and always will.

The Blues Begin

On a night in the year 1903, Mr. W. C. Handy, who later would come to be known as the "Father of the Blues," stood on a train station platform in Tutwiler, Mississippi, looking at his watch.

His train was nine hours late.

He gazed into the darkness, down the rails that ran through the middle of the small town. Wind blew through the trees. A dog barked. In a window, a shade was drawn shut. But no train, no whistle, no headlight. Muttering to himself, he snapped his watch shut, slipped it into his vest pocket, and settled down on a nearby bench. If the train was late, he might as well try to get some sleep, he thought.

He crossed his arms and closed his eyes.

Handy was, for all intents and purposes, an African-American aristocrat. Nattily dressed, a college-educated professional composer, he was the leader of a successful brass band that played at dances, funerals, and county fairs all over Mississippi. But the music his band played at these events was nothing like the music to which his name would become forever attached. Handy's band played the standard brass band selections of the time—marches, dirges, romantic ballads—and Handy aspired not to be an artistic innovator but simply to continue with his already flourishing, thoroughly

11

conventional musical career. After all, the steady money he made playing ho-hum tunes, such as "The Blue Danube Waltz" and "I'll Take You Home Again, Kathleen," kept him in the stylish clothes he preferred and helped him buy first-class train tickets. He couldn't make the trains run on time, that was obvious, but he was a fairly prosperous man.

His chin fell to his chest.

What woke him was not the sound of a train coming into the station. Instead, Handy encountered "the weirdest music" he'd ever heard.[1]

As Handy's eyes fluttered open, he saw a man in ragged clothes sitting at the other end of the bench, playing a guitar. This in itself was not an unusual sight in the rural South. Handy had probably seen hundreds of other black men in shabby clothes, playing the guitar at any time of day, on porches, street corners, or sitting on the back of a wagon in the middle of a field. What was different was the way the man was playing the guitar. Rather than strumming and picking the strings, the man was sliding an *open pocketknife* up and down the guitar's neck—making the notes bend and slide, the strings moan and wail. The sound was so much like a human voice that you could almost say the guitar was crying.

Listening to this amazing sound, Handy pulled a notebook out of his pocket and scribbled down, as best he could, the strange, writhing notes the man was playing.

And with that, the blues entered written history.

No one can say, though, that the blues were actually born that night. Only a few months earlier, Gertrude "Ma" Rainey, a professional vaudeville singer, could have told of a similiar experience she'd had while playing one night in a small Missouri town. At the time, she was touring with a musical revue called The Rabbit Foot Minstrels, and as she was preparing to go onstage, she heard a young woman singing a sad, mournful tune outside the vaudeville tent. Rainey stopped to listen to this woman's "strange and poignant" song—which was about how the young woman's man had left her—and, knowing that she'd never heard music quite like this, Rainey decided to work this novel song into her act.[2] And meanwhile, hundreds of miles away, over in Oklahoma City, a white violin player named Hart

Wand was playing a melody that an African-American employee of his father's said gave him "the blues."[3]

The blues were in the air.

But where did they really begin? Although Handy and Rainey had their hands in "discovering" the blues—and Wand his role in naming them—it's obvious that the music already existed in some form. For years the blues had already been played by African-Americans in bars, barns, and train stations all across the southern United States. It was only at the turn of the century that it was at last noticed by professional musicians and finally brought to wider attention.

So where did the blues begin?

For that, we have to go back to Africa.

In 1745, a book of travel writings called a *Collection of Voyages* contained the following description of life on the West Coast of Africa:

> Of the role of the musician in the society there seems to be considerable agreement, although there are differences in the name. Those who play on these instruments are persons of a very singular character, and seem to be their poets as well as their musicians. . . . The Kings and great men in the country keep two or more of these [musicians] to divert them and entertain foreigners on occasion.[4]

This passage refers to a well-known presence found in the tribes of West Africa: the *griot*. The griot was a kind of African wandering minstrel, traveling from village to village, playing songs, telling stories, spreading jokes, advice, and wisdom. Carrying an instrument that resembled a modern-day banjo, the griot was regarded as a kind of holy figure who was possessed of special knowledge and talents, someone whose funny songs had the power to make you laugh, and whose sad songs had the power to make you cry. The griot was, it could be said, a walking, talking circus and encyclopedia combined, capable of

Slaves dig sweet potatoes on a South Carolina plantation in 1862. Enslaved Africans brought the tradition of the work song with them to the United States.

both entertainment and enlightenment. Able to make you dance and think, the griot was an essential part of village life.

Almost every West African tribe—the Bantu, Wolof, Fula, Ewe, Akan, Mandingo, and Yoruba, to name only a few—had some kind of griot tradition. In the land that is now the countries of Nigeria, Senegal, Ghana, Sierra Leone, Liberia, the Ivory Coast, Togo, and Cameroon, this folk tradition, like many others, had been sustained for perhaps thousands of years. But West Africa was soon to be convulsed by the arrival of Europeans and the advent of the transatlantic slave trade. Ships from Europe, bound for America, appeared on the horizon, and their captains and sailors—carrying muskets, swords, and shackles—landed on the coast, walked up the beach in their strange clothes, looked around, and demanded slaves. A horrific chapter in human history had begun, and neither Africa nor America would be the same again.

Between the years 1505 and 1870, in the largest forced migration in human history, an estimated ten million Africans were captured and brought to the Americas. Among these were presumably a vast number of griots. But now rather than sing the old village songs, the griots invented new songs that addressed their new and terrifying circumstances: songs about being chained on ships below deck like animals, about those who did not survive the brutal crossing to the New World, about the homes they would never see again. And once in America, there were other hardships to sing about: the ignominy of the auction block, the separation of family members, the remorseless treatment at the hands of landowners. Although in those years most landowners attempted to suppress all signs of African culture, the slaves nevertheless hung on as best they could to whatever elements of their culture were still left to them, so as to carve out some place in the world that reflected their values and experiences. Principle among these surviving, tenacious cultural elements was the African emphasis on the importance of music in daily life.

By the end of the Civil War, African-Americans had blended African and European influences to create their own complete, and unique, culture. Like any society, this one was complex and diverse, and it included African-American styles of dance and storytelling, work and spirituality, conversation and community. By sifting among the many elements of this vibrant, life-sustaining world, we can trace the specific musical roots of what would be known, by the end of the century, as "the blues."

The Work Song

In West Africa most tribes sang songs as they worked. Planting, harvesting, weaving, preparing meals—each activity had a specific musical accompaniment. It is no wonder. Almost any repetitive, manual task seems much easier, and somehow more meaningful, when it is turned into a song—when the sound of a hoe striking the ground, for example, is not simply the sound of a hoe striking the ground, but is instead the rhythm track of a song you are singing. Consequently, it is not surprising that West Africans, when forced to work in the furnace-hot, backbreaking cotton fields of the American South, would continue this work song tradition.

Once in America, however, this tradition underwent a unique transformation. Rather than being a kind of celebration of work, as the West African songs had often been, the field songs of the Southern slaves became, in part, ones of lamentation and misery, of protest and complaint. The songs, often invented spontaneously while people were working in the fields and then passed on from generation to generation, dealt with the slaves' immediate concerns: the desire to escape, the hope for revenge, the yearning to be reunited with family members. At the time, many whites were fooled by the nature of these songs. Oddly enough, these whites thought that singing slaves were expressing their serenity, their acceptance of their hard lot in life. The black leader and former slave Frederick Douglass, however, wrote that these songs expressed just the opposite:

> I have often been utterly astonished, since I came North, to find persons who could speak of the singing among slaves as evidence of their contentment and happiness. It is impossible to conceive of a greater mistake. Slaves sing most when they are most unhappy. The songs of the slaves represent the sorrows of his life; and he is relieved by them only as an aching heart is relieved by its tears.[5]

The West African tradition of singing while working was serving the slave in good stead. Although the songs did not make the work any easier, they at least provided an outlet for expression, a way of transforming an unwanted experience into a personal vision. Unless he or she was willing to sacrifice his or her life, a slave could not openly or physically resist the masters who used chains, guns, and dogs to keep slaves in line. But through artistic creations, such as the work song, a slave could at least try to be psychologically free. Although forced to pick cotton, a slave could, in his or her imagination, run down the road and leave the the plantation and all its suffering. In the imagination, a slave could even be back in Africa once more. The master could control a slave's body, but the master could not control a slave's mind.

Sonny Terry, a blues harmonica master, summed up the importance of the work song this way:

> I'll tell you where the blues began. Back there working on them cotton farms, working hard and the man won't pay 'em so the people started singin', "Ohhh, I'm leaving one of these days and it won't be long." See what's happenin' is givin them the blues. "You gonna look for me one of these mornings and I'll be gone. Ohhh yeah!"[6]

And what about the word the "blues"?

By the middle of the nineteenth century, it had already become a slang word used to describe feelings of sadness and misery. Soldiers in the Civil War, for example, wrote home about how the horrors of war and the drudgery of army life were giving them "the blues." It makes sense then, that this word would one day be applied to these songs. It describes them all too well.

The Spiritual

The church was another important element of African-American life—and like so many other aspects of this culture, the black church was a distinctive blend of European influences and African-American concerns. Most slave owners felt it was necessary to impose Christianity on their slaves, believing that this would eradicate the slaves' "pagan" African beliefs, making them more "European," more "civilized," and thus, it was thought, easier to control. In large part, African-Americans did indeed embrace these Christian traditions, but not to the effect that slaveholders had hoped. Instead, African-Americans concentrated on those aspects of Christianity that most reflected their own dilemmas and desires. In the stories of the Old Testament, slaves found revealing parallels to their lives in America. They identified, for example, with the Hebrew slaves who longed to escape from Egypt and to return to their homeland of Israel; they felt a kinship with the humble David in his amazing triumph over the giant

17

Goliath. If we substitute in these instances "Africa" for "Egypt," and "the master" for "Goliath," it becomes quite clear why the slaves so often adopted the Christian church as their own.

The spiritual was one of the most potent expressions of African-American religious beliefs, and these spirituals, like African-American Christianity itself, came about through a blending of influences. Many had their basis in the standard hymns of the day. The works of the English composer Issac Watts, who wrote the music to "Amazing Grace," were particularly popular among black congregations, and it has been documented that an 1820 edition of Watts's hymns had wide circulation throughout the southern United States.[7] Building upon the melodic and verse structure of hymns, such as those written by Watts, black congregations began to create their own songs. An example of this kind of invention can be found in an excerpt from a monograph written by James Miller McKim, a white minister from Philadelphia who collected slave spirituals during the Civil War. In this excerpt, McKim interviews a slave who has been accused of stealing corn and who has been given a hundred lashes as punishment—an incident that gave rise to the creation of a new spiritual.

> I asked one of these blacks . . . where they got these songs. "Dey make em, sah." "How do they make them?" After a pause . . . he said, "I'll tell you; it's dis way. My master call me up and order me a short peck of corn and a hundred lash. My friends see it and is sorry for me. When dey come to de praise meeting dat night dey sing about it. Some's very good singers and know how; and dey work it in, work it in, you know' til they get it right; and dat's dey way. . . .

> *No more driver call me*
> *No more driver call*
> *No more driver call me*
> *Many thousands die!*
>
> *No more peck of corn for me*
> *No more peck of corn*

Christians prepare for their baptism in the Potomac River. Spirituals, deeply emotional religious songs, played an important role in the early development of the blues.

No more peck of corn for me
Many thousands die!

No more hundred lash for me
No more hundred lash
No more hundred lash for me
Many thousands die!

And so a spiritual was born. In this example, we can see in play many of the ideas we've been discussing concerning the development of the blues. Once more, African-Americans had taken a brutal fact of life—in this case, a beating consisting of a hundred lashes—and without in any way reducing the brutality of the event that sparked it, managed to create a work of art. In doing so these slaves had, in a certain sense, transcended the beating. This method of transforming experience would continue to be used by African-Americans long after this incident from the Civil War had passed—and as it became obvious, in the postwar years of Jim Crow, that the struggle for freedom was far from over.

The Professional Song

Before the end of the Civil War, an African-American who aspired to be a professional musician could usually only find work in the popular traveling minstrel shows that traveled throughout the North. Although the minstrel shows provided a musician with some performing experience, the audiences attending the minstrel shows were predominantly white, and despite the somewhat more enlightened attitudes toward race relations in the North, these audiences wished to be treated to the usual racial stereotypes expected from performing African-Americans. Given these restrictive circumstances, little music emerged from these shows that accurately reflected the African-American experience or added to the growth of the blues.

Following the war, however, there was a veritable explosion of African-American professional musicians who played to black, as well as white, audiences. While it's difficult to say what musical influence these performers may have had upon the development of the blues, that African-Americans began to play professionally to African-American audiences is of inestimable importance. These performers set an important precedent for up-and-coming musicians: they proved, among other things, that a life spent playing music written by blacks, and enjoyed by blacks, was indeed possible.

One of the brightest stars of these early black professionals was ragtime pianist and composer Scott Joplin. Born on November 24, 1868, most likely in Texarkana, Texas, Joplin's "Maple Leaf Rag" sold a remarkable one million print copies in 1899, the year of its release. With the money earned from this and his other successes—such as "The Entertainer," "Pine Apple Rag," and "The Ragtime Dance"—Joplin was able, for much of his life, to quit performing as an itinerant piano player and devote himself exclusively to teaching and composing. Gifted with perfect pitch, utterly disciplined in his approach to music, Joplin rightly considered himself to be a serious composer rather than a popular songwriter, as is plainly revealed by his full-length opera, *Treemonisha*. Although at the time of his death in 1917 Joplin had weathered devasting personal and financial travails, he had nevertheless sustained himself as a committed, professional musician throughout his life.

The unquestioned center of the burgeoning postwar black musical establishment, of which Joplin was a part, was New Orleans. This vibrant, culturally diverse city had a rich musical heritage—New Orleans could boast its own "Negro Philharmonic Society" in 1830—and its more relaxed attitude concerning race offered African-Americans a degree of freedom and possibilities for self-expression found nowhere else in the South.

By the turn of the century, New Orleans was literally alive with a wide range of African-American music: John Robichaux's Lyre Club Symphony Orchestra performed the standard classical repertory, the Excelsior Brass Band played popular tunes of the day, and innumerable other musicians entertained patrons in the city's thriving honky-tonks and cabarets. In New Orleans it was possible for a large number of African-Americans to make a living—however haphazard and day-to-day—simply by playing music. In other words, there was no place on earth like it.

With the perspective of some hundred years, it is no exaggeration to suggest that these heady years in New Orleans were the singularly most important ones in the history of American music. Consider this: it was there, at that time, that many of the musical foundations of jazz and the blues—and by extension rock 'n' roll, hip-hop, and rap—were created by such pioneering African-American musicians as Ferdinand "Jelly Roll" Morton, Sidney Bechet, Freddie Keppard, and Buddy Bolden. These now often overlooked innovators created styles of music that would eventually be heard in every corner of the world. Of course at the time there was no way of knowing how widespread and influential this music would become. But one thing was clear to ambitious black musicians at the turn of the century: New Orleans, dancing and swaying there at the mouth of the mighty Mississippi, was the place to

21

be. Get there on a boat, get there on a horse, get there on foot—just make sure you get there.

The Guitar

One instrument in particular helped give birth to the blues: the guitar. Although it is certainly interesting and constructive to consider all the various influences that led to the development of the blues, it's also important to keep in mind that the blues, first and last, are music, and so naturally have to be played on something. Somebody has to actually put fingers to a fretboard in order to create those sounds that people now identify with the blues. So let's take a look at this all-important instrument, and how blues musicians came to use it.

Although the guitar as we know it today had its origins in Europe, there is also a long African tradition of playing music on stringed instruments. Often these African instruments were quite simple. A strip of fiber, usually animal intestine, was strung from one end of a bowed piece of wood to the other. By plucking this string, and bending the bow, various sounds could be produced. More complicated creations along these lines had the string passing over a drum, so as to give more resonance to the tones produced. With a little imagination, it's easy to see how these instruments resembled a modern banjo. A banjo, after all, is just that: tightly strung strings passing over a hollow, drumlike soundboard. Having this sort of background, it's no wonder that early African-Americans found European-based instruments such as the guitar to be strangely familiar.

Besides these African forerunners, though, the guitar had two more qualities that made it particularly useful to early blues musicians. A guitar was *affordable* and *portable*. It didn't cost all that much, and you could carry it along with you, no matter where you went. Considering the difficult living conditions of early African-Americans, this made the guitar very attractive. Living in poverty, an elaborate instrument such as a piano was clearly too expensive to be had; and because slaves could never be sure where they might be living next, the guitar was an instrument that could easily be thrown onto the back of a

A banjo player strums a tune.

wagon, strapped to the side of a mule, or carried in your hand, depending on where you were going.

As with so many other aspects of European culture, African-Americans adopted the guitar and then adapted it according to African influences, creating something uniquely their own. This is particularly true in the way that early blues musicians *played* the guitar. If you look closely at the neck of an average guitar, you'll see that it is divided into 21 separate sections. Each section is separated from the other by a thin metal bar called a *fret*. The space between each fret corresponds to a single note. European and white guitar players always paid strict attention to the frets of a guitar, and as a result played notes that followed standard Western scales. Early blues musicians, however, with their African background, approached the guitar in a totally different way. Since stringed African instruments didn't have frets, African musicians usually created their sounds by bending the entire bowed instrument while sliding something across the string. By bending and sliding over a fretless string, *gliding* instead of *jumping* from one note to another, African musicians played notes that simply didn't exist in Western scales—those being the ones that lay *between* standard Western notes.

This African approach—that of sometimes ignoring the positions of the frets—revolutionized guitar playing. Even today, one of the most distinctive traits of a blues guitarist is to bend one of the guitar strings while playing. Next time you get a chance, pay close attention when someone plays a guitar: if he or she bends the strings, creating that unmistakable blues cry, then he or she is following in the footsteps of ancient African musicians.

Early blues musicians, again following African tradition and ignoring the usually all-important frets, also created an entirely new sound by sliding a broken bottleneck, a knife, or any other suitable piece of material, along the string. This created a sound similar to a bent string, but was even more radical. Rather than just bending one note at a time, a musician could now slide through an entire scale. In fact, this method is now called—simply enough—playing the *slide guitar*. Today, specially made, usually ceramic or metal, slides are made to slip over the guitarist's fingers. Nobody has to use broken bottles or knives anymore, but the idea is exactly that of the early blues musicians.

We usually don't think of the blues and country-western music having much to do with one another. But, if you notice, many country-western bands include a musician playing a *lap steel* guitar. This is a guitar, which, as the name suggests, lays flat so it can be placed in your lap—and it is *always* played in the manner of a slide guitar. Once you hear its distinctive sliding twang, you'll recognize it as being one of the standard instruments in the country-western lineup. Although the lap steel is pure country-western in sound, its heritage is full of the blues.

These, then, are the musical roots of the blues. It was from this union of work songs, spirituals, and professional songs that the "weirdest music" he'd ever heard came to W. C. Handy on that lonesome night in Tutwiler.

One last thing, though, should not be overlooked. In considering the history of the blues, it is tempting to concentrate on the various social factors mentioned here, such as slavery and its eventual demise, that obviously influenced the development of this music. Without question, the social conditions of African-Americans had an enormous impact on the creation of the blues, but there remains a much more elusive, and yet just as important, element. That is the element of individual artistry. Because so much blues history has gone unrecorded it is easy to forget that for every accountable social factor there was also an unknown, individual artist responsible for the creation of the blues. For example: Who was the first person to slide a pocketknife along the neck of a guitar? Who was the first person to sing a song of protest in a field? Who was the first griot to come to America? Someone actually did all these things. Someone actually played these roles and thus made an inestimable contribution to the history of music. But his or her name will never be known. The best we can do is to acknowledge that we have been the beneficiaries of their talents and innovations.

The Early Years: In the Country

As the story of the blues goes along, we'll see that its history falls, more or less, into two categories: "country" blues and "city" blues. Before we look at more blues history, though, it will be worth our while to first get a little more familiar with these two aspects of the blues.

Without question, the blues began in the rural part of the American South known as the Mississippi Delta. The Delta is that broad, flat expanse of land that runs along either side of the southern half of the Mississippi River. Beginning in the southeastern corner of Missouri and the southwestern corner of Tennessee, the delta continues all the way down to where the Mississippi empties into the Gulf of Mexico. Mile for mile, acre for acre, more inspired blues musicians have come from this stretch of land than any other part of the world. Although the music that these musicians played is known by various names—"country" blues, "folk" blues, "delta" blues—all of these are used simply to describe that music that developed in this rural setting. This music, created as it was by usually self-taught musicians, is often rough, hard-edged, and raw. It is usually played on standard, rather than electric, instruments.

The city blues are, obviously, the counterpart of the country blues. Sometimes known as "urban" blues, this is the name given to the music that developed in large, metropolitan areas. The city of Chicago, Illinois, played such an important part in the development of the urban blues that they are sometimes simply called "Chicago" blues. As blacks began to migrate from the rural South to large, industrialized northern cities in the early years of the twentieth century, they brought their music with them—thus, urban blues are a modification of the music that began in the countryside. Today, the urban blues sound usually refers to that music made famous by Chicago musicians such as Muddy Waters, who, in the mid-1950s and early 1960s, began playing the blues through electric guitars and amplifiers.

Obviously, this gets us a little ahead of the game. We've hardly left the very beginnings of the blues, and now we're already talking about what became of them some half century later. Nevertheless, as you continue to read, it will be helpful to keep these two categories—country blues and city blues—in mind, so that the next time you hear some blues music, you can decide which category it belongs to. It is important to remember, though, that country blues styles and city blues styles influenced one another in hundreds of different, subtle ways, and separating them into these two categories in some ways simplifies what is an infinitely more rich and complex subject.

Still, a few signposts along the way never hurt.

So, to begin with, the country blues . . .

The early years of this century were painful ones for most blacks living in the American South. Slavery was gone, but a racist white society continued to oppress blacks. Lynchings were common; schools, neighborhoods, and jobs were strictly segregated; and most blacks continued to be tied to the land because of the insidiously merciless system of land and labor management known as sharecropping.

A sharecropper worked for a landowner and in return was given a small wage, a place to live, and space for a small garden. As part of this agreement, however, the sharecropper also had to buy whatever goods he or she might need throughout the year—food, clothing, medicine, and so on—from the landowner, the cost of which was deducted from the sharecropper's wages. Thus at the end of the year, because of the low wages and the exorbitant prices landowners charged for such supplies, the sharecropper found himself in debt to the landowner. To pay off this debt, the sharecropper was required to continue to work the land—for an even smaller wage. Thus a vicious cycle of poverty and dependence was created. Year after year the sharecropper found himself deeper in debt to the landowner, with the hope of paying off this rising debt becoming dimmer with each passing month. So the sharecropper continued to work in the flat, sun-baked, humid fields of the South, picking cotton, pushing a plow, and nursing wounds.

It is no wonder that many sharecroppers packed up their belongings in the middle of the night and fled. Yet if caught, the sharecropper was sure to be imprisoned. And if the sharecropper managed to avoid imprisonment, where could one hope to go? To find work one would have to find another landowner, where the cycle of work and debt would simply begin all over again.

Many African-Americans sought to escape the bonds of sharecropping by finding work on railroads, by moving to more industrialized cities, by trying to save enough money to begin businesses, or by finding solace in the traditions of the church. Others found their paths of escape through the blues.

Charley Patton

Charley Patton was one of the earliest known blues masters. Born in 1891 in Bolton, Mississippi—the middle of share-cropping country—to a sharecropping family, Patton was restless, eager to leave the sharecropper's life behind and to find the kind of freedom that the racist South did not allow blacks. Growing up on a series of farms, Patton was exposed to the local music, those melodies and rhythms Handy was soon to call the blues, as it was played by men on front porches, in back rooms, and down on the banks of the river. No doubt its expressive power greatly

Early blues master Charley Patton (1891–1942)

appealed to him. When playing the blues, Patton found, you could say all the things you felt, no matter what the rich and privileged landowner might think. Through the blues, he found, he could be free.

As a young man, Patton had taught himself to play guitar by watching the older musicians who lived around him. Soon he was playing the blues, at first making a meager living as a traveling musician. He went from town to town up and down the Mississippi River, playing his guitar at dances and fairs, in taverns and juke joints, and, thanks to his obvious musical gifts, he became a widely known and popular entertainer. In almost every way, Patton was beginning to succeed in escaping the sharecropper's plight of being tied to the land: as his popularity rose, he traveled even farther afield, from Georgia to Texas, New Orleans to Memphis, St. Louis to Chicago. By the end of his life—he suffered a fatal heart attack at the age of forty-three—Patton had become financially comfortable thanks to his endless touring and, later, the success of his recordings. He married eight times, filled himself with the adventures of the road, and led a life of personal independence that would have been unimaginable to his ancestors. His talent and hard work had been recognized and rewarded.

As a musician, Patton was a true innovator. More than likely, he was the first person to transform what was essentially a folk music tradition into a means of intensely individual expression. No one had ever played the blues quite the way Charlie Patton played them. The complexity of his guitar playing was, up to that time, unparalleled. In addition to picking the strings, Patton snapped them with the thumb of his right hand while creating whining sounds by bending the strings with the forefingers of his left. Likewise, the lyrics he wrote possessed a passion and clarity of emotion rarely heard from any previous single performer. And many agree that Patton's words are, in fact, his most vibrant artistic tool. In his raw-edged voice one can plainly, painfully hear his intense desire to escape, as well as the open rage Patton felt toward the racist institutions of the South.

I'm going away to a world unknown.
I'm going away to a world unknown.
I'm worried now, but I won't be worried long. . . .

Every day seem like murder here.
Every day seem like murder here.
I'm gonna leave tomorrow. I know you don't bit
more care.[1]
　　　　　　　　　—"Down the Dirt Road Blues"

Although Patton led too varied a life to suggest that it could be summed up in just a few words, these lyrics serve as a testament to the main themes of his life. He was bound and determined to leave behind the oppressed sharecroppers' existence, even if this led him to a "world unknown." He was more than willing to tell the truth about the brutal conditions that most African-Americans lived in: "Every day seem like murder here." And regardless of how insignificant the landowners had tried to make him feel—"I know you don't bit more care"—he would make his own way in the world. He was, in fact, going to "leave tomorrow." You'd better look quick, he seemed to say, because if you wait another second, Charley Patton will be long, long gone. And he'll be in a better place than you can ever imagine.

Blind Lemon Jefferson

Believe it or not, his name really was Lemon.

Born blind to Alec and Classie Jefferson in the summer of 1897, outside of the dusty town of Wortham, Texas, Lemon Jefferson was to become another one of the early blues greats. Alec and Classie, though, were worried early on about their pudgy, sightless son. How was a blind black boy ever going to make it? He obviously couldn't farm, work the railroads, or find employment in any of the other occupations usually held by blacks. Who was going to give their child the help he would need once they were gone? A clue to his future lay in one of the boy's unusual characteristics: though blind and heavy, he could chase and catch the chickens on his parents' farm. By listening to the sound of the chicken's scratching and scampering feet, he could reason the direction they were headed. Amazed by the boy's apparently extraordinary sense of hearing, the Jefferson family and their neighbors looked on one day as Lemon grabbed a running chicken, holding it up by its legs, smiling in triumph.[2]

And so it was this heightened sensitivity to sound that helped Lemon Jefferson find a place in Wortham. No one knows who first taught him the rudiments of guitar playing, but by the time he was fourteen Lemon was playing, remarkably well, in front of the Wortham feed store, an upturned hat in front of him for contributions from passers-by. Overweight and earnest, wearing a useless pair of glasses over his eyes, Lemon attracted a great deal of attention. Soon he was playing at fairs, picnics, and dances all over the county. It seemed as though despite the bad cards he'd been dealt, Lemon was creating a job for himself after all. He was becoming an accomplished entertainer.

He probably never knew that back in Africa, blind children often became singing, storytelling griots. In Africa it was considered quite natural that blind children, because they could not do most of the other village tasks, should become performers. Although he had no way of knowing that he was maintaining this ancient tradition, Lemon was convinced that music was his future. And so at the age of twenty, he said good-bye to his family and the town of Wortham, determined to make a name for himself in the big city of Dallas, some eighty miles away.

The move to Dallas would prove to be Lemon's windfall and, in many ways, his undoing.

In Dallas, Lemon naturally gravitated toward the city's red-light district, the place where a musician could most likely find work. Although he continued to play the streets, Lemon soon became a fixture in the city's cabarets, brothels, and taverns. Weighing in at some two hundred and fifty pounds, Lemon would prop his imposing figure on a chair in the corner of a honky-tonk and play all night, gazing at the the darkness in

Blind Lemon Jefferson (1897–1929),
one year before his death.

front of him. When he couldn't find work in the honky-tonks, he wrestled in theaters. He was billed as the amazing blind wrestler. These wrestling performances were strictly a novelty act, bringing Lemon as many jeers and hoots from the audiences as they did money, but when the music jobs were scarce, wrestling kept him in room and board. It also paid for the beer, wine, and whiskey upon which he was increasingly dependent. In the rough-and-tumble world of Dallas, Lemon was becoming an alcoholic.

Nevertheless, his musical star, in contrast to his increasingly reckless personal life, continued to rise. He began to tour the South with a number of popular musical shows, including one with Charley Patton, and in 1924 his life changed forever. By this time, record companies had discovered that there was a large African-American audience for the blues, and most had launched divisions devoted exclusively to producing what were patronizingly known as "race" records. A scout for Paramount Records, based out of Chicago, "discovered" Lemon in Dallas and immediately offered him a recording contract. Lemon leapt at the chance. He packed up his belongings and, under the direction of Paramount, moved to Chicago. It was there that he made his name. Thanks to his recordings, he briefly became one of the most famous blues musicians in the country.

Lemon's first record, featuring his "Long Lonesome Blues" and "Got the Blues," was an instant hit. No other "country blues"—that is, a blues song featuring only guitar and voice, in the style of most rural musicians—had sold nearly as well. As Lemon continued to release hit after hit for Paramount from 1926 to 1929, his success no doubt opened the door for many other country blues singers. The precedent he set was, in fact, probably his most significant contribution to the development of the blues. His music, unlike Patton's for example, was not particularly innovative. Likewise, he rarely expressed the emotions of deep, personal rage that Patton did—a fact that probably contributed to his success in the white recording establishment. Lemon seemed to be content singing what were becoming known as "woman-done-me-wrong" songs—songs that were commercially effective but artistically repetitive.

It is hard to tell, however, to what extent Lemon's chronic alcoholism was influencing his output. Those who knew Lemon during his time in Chicago report that, for the most part, his principal concern seemed to be not pursuing any particular artistic or professional goal but simply to have enough money to keep up his drinking habit. And the executives at Paramount were not above manipulating Lemon in this matter: rather than paying him the portion of recording profits he deserved, they often compensated him with liquor. The destructive pattern he'd created for himself in Dallas followed him to Chicago. If Lemon had not suffered from alcoholism, he may have gone on to achieve even greater things. But this much is certain: the most successful blues player of the time was dying inside.

Lemon's end came suddenly. On a snowy Chicago night, sometime during the winter of 1929–30, Lemon left the Paramount recording studios bound for a house party. The next morning he was found in a snowbank, frozen, his guitar at his side. Exactly what happened the night before is anybody's guess. Some say Lemon made it to the house party, where he got drunk, and then left. Some say he never arrived at all. Paramount attributed his death to a heart attack. Others said the blind man had lost his way in the streets and had simply frozen to death. Whatever the cause, Blind Lemon Jefferson was dead.

In the course of his career, Lemon recorded only one song with plainly religious overtones. "See That My Grave Is Kept Clean" has as its chorus:

> *Well there's only kind favor I ask of you,*
> *One kind favor I ask of you,*
> *Lord, there's one kind favor I ask of you,*
> *Please see that my grave is kept clean.*

The favor was not to be granted. Lemon's body was returned to his hometown of Wortham, where he was buried in the cemetery on the outskirts of town. The grave, however, went unmarked, and today nobody knows if Lemon's grave is clean.

Robert Johnson

Among blues musicians, an aura of fascination and mystery surrounds Robert Johnson, one unlike any other. This enigmatic sense has developed for a number of reasons. The facts of his life remain sketchy; he died young after leading a nomadic life, poisoned by a jealous husband; he was quiet, shy, an intense loner; and his phenomenal musical skills, some say, were the result of a pact he'd made with the devil. Sifting through the details of Robert Johnson's life and listening to his recordings is like tracing the footprints of a ghost. Just when you think you've figured out where he is going, and why, he disappears, and you know less about him than when you began. No doubt this is how Johnson would have wanted it.

Most blues historians, however, agree that Robert Johnson may have been the greatest blues musician who ever lived.

He was born in Hazlehurst, Mississippi, on May 8, 1911. His mother, Julia Major Dodds, was married to Charles Dodds, who'd been forced to leave Hazlehurst in 1909 under threat of death from local landowners, who claimed he owed them money. In Charles Dodds's absence, Julia, still married, had a brief romance with a plantation worker named Noah Johnson. Their union produced one child, Robert. Taking her other children along, Julia then moved with Robert from farm to farm, from work camp to work camp, trying to keep her tattered family together.

No doubt this troubled family life had a lasting effect upon the young Robert. Neither his natural father, Noah, or stepfather, Charles, wanted to acknowledge Robert or help him in any way. This sense of rejection may account for Johnson's predilection for using various aliases throughout his life. At different times he called himself R. L. Spencer, Robert Spencer, as well as many other names. Once he adopted the name Johnson, he falsely claimed to be a relative of Lonnie Johnson, another famous blues guitarist. It was almost as if he believed that by using these false names and false family connections, he could reinvent himself, could give himself the personal recognition that he did not receive in real life. And his home troubles did not end with childhood. At nineteen he married a sixteen-year-old woman who died during childbirth. Doubtless, this sorrow pursued him for the rest of his life.

It was about this time, at the age of nineteen or twenty, that Johnson began playing the guitar. Like Charlie Patton and Blind Lemon Jefferson before him, Robert was trying to escape and transform his troubled life by playing the blues.

Unlike Patton or Jefferson, however, Robert had a definite mentor—a person who, more than anyone else, taught him how to play. This was the legendary Eddie "Son" House. In a longer book, House would deserve a chapter devoted solely to his work, but for our purposes it is enough to say that if Robert Johnson had wanted a more accomplished teacher, he could not have found one. Under House's tutelage, Johnson learned the basics of blues guitar, as well as more advanced techniques. Johnson quickly absorbed all House had to teach him, and soon, as so often happens with a gifted student, he began to surpass House in some elements of his playing. This delighted House, who encouraged Johnson to take his music seriously and to become a professional musician, which Johnson did, with startling results.

Like most blues musicians of the time, Johnson began traveling the South, roaming from town to town, playing any place he could. He hitched rides on trains, rode on the backs of pickup trucks, or got enough money together for a bus ticket. He was always on the move, always restless, always moving on to where he hoped to find his next gig. Everywhere he went, he was remembered for his extraordinary playing and his strangely charismatic personality. Every person he met seemed to have a different, sometimes contradictory, memory of him: he was described variously as "an awful friendly guy," "shy," "tidy," "childish," "blunt," "moody," and "reckless."[3] There was one characteristic, however, that those who knew him agreed upon: he was there one minute and gone the next. You never knew when or where Robert Johnson was going to show up or when he was going to leave. It was as if he were on the run, as if he were being hunted down by something or

A rapt Eddie "Son" House (1902–88) bends
some mean notes at the 1965 Newport Folk Festival.
House taught Robert Johnson how
to play the blues.

someone no one else could see—and if he stayed too long in one place, he was going to get caught.

It may have been this "on the run" feeling he gave off that contributed to one of the persistent rumors surrounding Johnson: that he had gained his shocking musical talent in exchange for selling his soul to devil. He had to keep moving, it was said, because the devil himself was chasing him down, ready to take his soul. Less fancifully, there's no doubt that Johnson's musical prowess had come from an innate talent, discipline, and from House's wise teaching. Nevertheless, the rumor is an example of the strange effect he had on those around him.

By the mid-1930s, when Johnson was in his twenties, the market for blues records had already been well established. It had been ten years since Blind Lemon Jefferson had shown, beyond any question, that there was money to be made by producing records for black audiences. Record company scouts continued to keep watch for new performers, hoping to find, and sign a contract with, the next blues sensation. In what probably was the late summer or fall of 1936, Ernie Oertle, a scout for the American Record Company, met Robert Johnson and asked him to come to San Antonio, Texas, in November. He wanted Robert to make some records.

Johnson was thrilled. This was the opportunity he'd worked for all his life. He went to San Antonio, and there, over the course of three days, he made a series of recordings that alone would have assured him a place in blues history. In June of the next year, he went to Dallas for another American Record Company session. In a sweltering warehouse cooled only by electric fans blowing across blocks of ice, Johnson produced material that perhaps surpassed the quality of those first recordings. The blues would never be the same.

What was it about Robert Johnson's music that so entranced, and continues to entrance, so many people? Although he was a wildly proficient musician, there were at the time more technically sophisticated guitar players, such as Lonnie Johnson, to whom Robert claimed false kinship. Likewise, there were more practiced, more professional singers and songwriters. Yet with Robert Johnson these abilities—guitar playing, singing, and songwriting—came together in an utterly unrivaled manner. With this triad of talents, Johnson's music grips the listener with an emotional intensity that is unforgettable. To understand the power of Johnson's work, let's take a closer look at one of his songs: his version of Son House's earlier "Preachin' the Blues (Up Jumped the Devil)."

The song begins with a standard blues introduction. Suddenly Johnson leaps into a rapid, wailing, slide guitar theme. This theme alone sets the song apart from most blues motifs simply because of the incredible speed with which it is played. To modern ears, early blues music can sometimes sound unsettlingly slow, but "Preachin' the Blues" moves rapidly, propulsively, fueled by the barely restrained, nervous energy of Johnson's playing. Soon Johnson's high, keening tenor voice enters the mix, floating above the guitar, describing a bizarre, metaphorical transformation, wherein "the blues" has taken on a human form.

> I's up this mornin'
> ah, blues walkin' like a man
> I's up this mornin'
> ah, blues walkin' like a man

Does this mean that Robert Johnson isn't a man at all— that he is instead the ghostly spirit of the blues, having momentarily assumed the shape of a man? Or does this describe a fantastic encounter he has had, wherein he gets up in the morning and sees the blues walking down the road toward him like a man? Johnson doesn't pause to explain. The music propels him along so fast there's no time for explanation. The one sure thing is the pain and fear in Johnson's haunted, almost childlike voice. Then, after a brief musical passage in which Johnson simply speaks the phrase "worried blues. . .," his high voice drops at least an octave and delivers:

> . . . give me your right hand.[4]

His voice, no longer high, has become a guttural croak. It is deep, maniacal, zealous. He sounds like an imp speaking from the depths of hell. And the obscurity of the lyrics only increases this pervasive sense of dread. There is perhaps no more starkly terrifying moment in the entire repertoire of the blues than when Johnson speaks these simple words. Are "the blues" asking Robert Johnson for his right hand—or, more frighteningly, is Robert Johnson asking for *your* right hand? By the time you think you have an answer, Johnson and his music have moved on again and are already asking more questions, as if to say: you'll never catch up with me.

In all, this musical passage, from the opening of the song to this disorienting point, takes just 46 seconds. There is not a moment in all of Bach, Beethoven, or Mozart that is as dire as this.

"Preachin' the Blues (Up Jumped the Devil)" was probably too dire, too apocalyptic, for the tastes of the American Record Company executives, but they released it nevertheless. Ten other songs—songs infinitely easier on the ear, such as "Terraplane Blues" and "Kindhearted Woman"—were thought to have commercial appeal and were released as well. Following these recording sessions, Johnson returned to the Mississippi area, where he continued to travel and play as he had before. Now that his records were being circulated, however, he was becoming much more well known. His ability to enjoy this growing fame would nevertheless be short-lived. Like Blind Lemon Jefferson, Robert Johnson was to face an early, untimely death.

Although the exact circumstances remain in question, this much is known: On a night in August 1938, Johnson was playing at a dance in Three Forks, Mississippi. At some point during the evening, a man poisoned Johnson, believing rightly or wrongly that Johnson was flirting with his wife. By 1:00 A.M that night, Johnson was complaining that he felt sick, although he insisted he was well enough to continue playing. By 2:00 A.M. he was too sick to play and was carried to the town of Greenwood, where he apparently lay desperately ill for a

*Robert Johnson (1911–38), "King of the Delta Blues,"
in the mid-1930s*

number of days. He died on August 16, and—like too many other blues musicians—was buried in an unmarked grave in a small cemetery on the edge of town.

The obsession with death that pervaded Johnson's songs had reached its self-predicted end.

There was one final ironic twist relating to his death. John Hammond, a well-known supporter of African-American music, had been putting together in New York City what was to become an historical musical offering. Billed as "From Spirituals to Swing" and scheduled for performance at Carnegie Hall on December 23, 1938, the production was organized to present the best of African-American music— gospel, jazz, and the blues—to a wider audience. Hammond believed that Johnson was the finest blues musician alive and had wanted him to appear at this concert. Hammond contacted Ernie Oertle, who soon learned that Johnson was dead. Big Bill Broonzy took Johnson's place in the show, and Hammond played a recording of "Preachin' the Blues" as a tribute. The audience that night heard those chilling words—"give me your right hand"—but fame, unlike death, had come too late for Robert Johnson.

Meanwhile, in the City

*F*or most African-Americans at this time, conditions in the cities were not necessarily easier. They were just different. Rather than having to answer to the landowner, you had to answer to the landlord. Although not tied to the land as the sharecroppers were, blacks in the city nevertheless had to work against paltry wages, segregation, and the continuing threat of violent racism. In the first half of this century, for example, the phrase "race riot" had an entirely different connotation than it does today. It was at this time, in large northern cities such as Detroit and Chicago, that gangs of racist whites swarmed into black neighborhoods, destroying property, threatening residents, and attempting to instill fear in the black population. And while it is true that an African-American middle class—made up of lawyers, doctors, businesspeople, and artisans—had grown in the cities, these well-off, middle-class blacks nevertheless remained exceptions to the rule. Likewise, the middle class was no more immune to the laws of segregation and the specter of racism than were the poor.

Yet despite these trying circumstances, urban African-Americans developed their own sustaining, life-affirming culture. And as in the country, one of the central elements of this vibrant culture was music.

The style of urban music was in marked contrast, however, to that found in the country. In the country, the music was mostly informal, often based around roaming individuals, such as Charley Patton, Blind Lemon Jefferson, and Robert Johnson. The city, however, had a much more organized musical establishment in which African-Americans played the part of performers. In the city there were cigar-puffing record producers, watch-chain-wearing booking agents, and pin-striped theater owners, all of whom were looking to make a buck off popular talent. The famous Memphis-based Theater Owners Booking Association, known as T.O.B.A. and nicknamed Toby Time, maintained a circuit of performance stops throughout the eastern half of the United States, from St. Louis to Baltimore, New Orleans to New York. Doing "Toby Time" could be a musician's means of achieving some kind of financial security. To be picked up by T.O.B.A., though, meant a musician had to maintain a degree of reliable professionalism—and, more importantly, proven commercial appeal—frequently unknown to more isolated, rural musicians.

Because of these strictly commercial concerns, the urban sound was closely based upon mainstream, vaudeville songs—much more so than were the country blues. This does not mean that music in the city was less inventive. The city simply wasn't the origin of this new thing called "the blues," and so it took some time for the songwriters there—W. C. Handy, for example—to recognize its attraction and importance. Once the importance of the blues was recognized, however, urban musicians quickly absorbed it into their repertoire, altered their songs, and thus forever transformed American popular music.

Louis Armstrong

Louis Armstrong, one of the true geniuses of American music, was born on July 4, 1900, in New Orleans, in the midst of desperate, destructive poverty. Raised by his grandmother—his parents separated shortly after his birth—his entire wardrobe usually consisted of a pair of pants and one or two shirts. He often went barefoot, wandering through the dirty, rat-run alleys of the New Orleans ghetto where he lived, scavenging food out of garbage cans. When he could, he sold newspapers and delivered coal. Deprived of almost every imaginable material and psychological comfort, he was witness in this snarled maze of tenement houses, railroad tracks, and brothels to drug addiction, prostitution, and murder. Young Louis Armstrong lived as close to the edge as anyone could, either before or since. In the words of jazz historian James Lincoln Collier, "it is not startling that he grew up to be wealthy and celebrated, but that he grew up at all."[1]

Because he was living in the African-American section of New Orleans at the turn of the century, Armstrong could not help but be exposed to music: band music spilled out of dance halls, the flourishes of a piano player echoed down the street, someone sang and played a banjo on a wrought-iron balcony. Everywhere you went there was music. Yet Armstrong, however much he may have loved what he heard, was too poor to afford an instrument. He stood in doorways and watched the drummers, the guitar players, the trombone players, imagining what he might be able to do if he could just get one those instruments in his hand. The most he could do was sing for spare change with his friends in a street corner barbershop quartet.

The events of New Year's Day 1913 were to change his life forever. In New Orleans, it was traditional to celebrate New Year's Day in a big way: with daylong parties, fireworks, and shots fired in the air. Joining in the revelry, Louis slipped a gun out of his stepfather's house and, at the urging of friends, fired it above his head. Much to his surprise, a New Orleans policeman put a heavy hand on his shoulder. Not much impressed with Louis's high spirits, the policeman arrested him for vagrancy and possession of a firearm—and on the judge's order Louis was removed from his family and sent to the Colored Waifs' Home.

This may have been an unnecessarily harsh punishment for a minor crime, but ironically, as Armstrong acknowledged later in life, it was perhaps the best thing that could have happened to him. The Waifs' Home had a small brass band,

and Louis was given a cornet to play. No one would have guessed it at the time, but the world of jazz was soon to know a giant.

From his beginnings with the student band, Louis showed startling talent. Though he had no previous musical training—and it is unusual for a virtuoso of Armstrong's caliber to start playing at the relatively late age of fourteen—he instantly impressed the Waifs' Home music teacher, Peter Davis. Davis, recognizing Louis's unusual ability, gave him special attention, making him the leader of the school band and impressing upon him the essential elements of music and cornet playing. By the time Louis left the Waifs' Home three years later, he was already on his way to becoming a competent professional.

Once he had a cornet in his hand, there was no stopping Armstrong. Despite the occasional setbacks faced by any aspiring musician, Armstrong's popularity grew as he continued to master his art. Switching to the trumpet—an instrument at the time often considered to be the sole province of white classical musicians—Armstrong was called to Chicago to join the celebrated band of Joseph "King" Oliver as its principal brass player. In Chicago, Armstrong had the same success playing with Oliver as he'd had in New Orleans. Wherever Oliver's band played, the numbers that featured Armstrong's distinctive, bell-like playing were invariably the audience's favorites. As he bowed to wildly cheering and applauding crowds, it was plain that Armstrong had a gift larger than that of simply being another member of a band. He was ready to strike out on his own.

On November 12, 1925, Louis Armstrong and a group of musicians he had assembled—sometimes called the "Hot Five" and sometimes the "Hot Seven," depending on who was playing—walked into the Chicago recording studios of Okeh Records. When he was done making some five dozen cuts, the recordings Armstrong had produced were so strong and so original that they would forever leave their mark on the history of the blues and jazz. These recordings, as well as those that Armstrong continued to make throughout the 1920s and 1930s, were plainly unlike any made before, and their influence upon other musicians is inestimable.

47

Louis Armstrong's Hot Five in Chicago in 1925. The band featured Armstrong (1900–71) on trumpet and piano, Johnny St. Cyr on banjo, Johnny Dobbs on clarinet and sax, Kid Ory on trombone, and Lil Hardin Armstrong on piano.

Why was Armstrong's music so special?

The primary reason is that Armstrong entirely redefined the role of the solo in popular music. Until Armstrong, it was customary for solos in popular music to be brief and relatively uninspiring. Meant only to simply provide variety to the music, the solo was not supposed to be particularly important. The strength of Armstrong's playing changed all of this. His playing was so extraordinary, so moving, that he was simply better than almost any other musician in any other band. Armstrong's ability and musical inventiveness so soared above that of other musicians that it was only natural audiences came just to see him.

Today, the role of the soloist is such a common part of popular music that it seems as though it has always been that way. Muddy Waters, Miles Davis, John Coltrane, Jimi Hendrix, B. B. King, Eric Clapton—all of these musicians attracted, and in the case of King and Clapton still attract, attention not because of their band but because of their own solo work in front of the band. Likewise, in every rock video, there is almost always a point in the song where the lead guitarist takes his or her solo. Louis Armstrong started all of this.

Armstrong's own solos were distinctive principally because of his command of melody and of all the emotions that a strong melody can create in a listener. Armstrong adapted his playing to express whatever emotion was most appropriate to the song. He could be mischievious and joyful in "Sugar Foot Stomp," tender and loving in "Basin Street Blues," or sorrowful and haunted in "St. James Infirmary." Like Shakespeare, who created comedy and tragedy and good and evil characters all at the same time, Armstrong could express an almost inexhaustible range of emotions. Even in the course of the same song, such as the famous "West End Blues," Armstrong articulates widely different feelings—in this case, those of quiet desperation and absolute triumph. It has been said that listening to an Armstrong solo is like listening to an expert storyteller. You can hear him speaking to you, making you feel hope, fear, and suspense; making you doubt what is going to happen next; making you doubt if he will ever be able to lift his spirits again. Finally, when you least expect it, he gives you a happy ending—all with a single trumpet.

None of this was an accident. Naturally gifted and highly skilled, Armstrong was a consummate musician, perfectly in control of every aspect of his craft and completely aware of what he was doing.

To the annoyance of some music critics and musicians, Armstrong did not continue expanding the range of his playing after these formative decades. The advent of be-bop—bringing with it the stunning talents of Dizzy Gillespie, Charlie Parker, Miles Davis, and John Coltrane, all of whom reinvented entire categories of jazz—did not seem to interest Armstrong. Instead he appeared to be content repeating himself. From time to time, he even laid his trumpet down, making his name as a popular singer of such emotionally sterile songs as "Mack the Knife" and "Hello, Dolly." Unfortunately, many people identify him with this later, immensely popular and lucrative phase of his career, unaware that in his time he was a singularly influential American musician.

Rightly or wrongly, Armstrong considered himself to be more of an entertainer than an artist. All the things that eventually brought him jabs from the critics—his comic antics, his singing, his selection of less-than-sophisticated material—had in fact been part of his act since his early days in New Orleans. Armstrong aimed to please, and please he did.

Gertrude "Ma" Rainey

We've met Ma Rainey before. She was the one, back in 1902, who heard the unknown Missouri girl singing that "strange and poignant" song.

On the night she heard it, Rainey was already in the midst of a successful career as a vaudeville singer. Because of her success, she had little incentive to work the blues into her shows. She made her living as an entertainer, and so it was important that she keep her audiences happy, giving them what they came to see. At this time, the blues—it would still be some sixteen years before the first blues record was to be released—had no proven audience appeal. Nevertheless, Rainey took a risk, and the rest, as the saying insists, is history.

She was born Gertrude Pridgett in Columbus, Georgia, in 1886. By the age of fourteen she was already performing in a local minstrel show—a show called, with self-conscious comic design, "A Bunch of Blackberries."[2] Four years later, roughly about the time she first worked the blues into her act, she married William "Pa" Rainey, an older entertainer. Taking on the nickname of "Ma," she and William Rainey struck out on their own as a song-and-dance team. Through the summer and fall, with Ma doing the singing and Pa doing the dancing, they traveled the rural South wherever farm work was being done—the hard-pressed sharecroppers were always eager for some kind of entertainment—and in the winter they usually found jobs in New Orleans. It was there that Gertrude Rainey worked with a number of the country's best musicians: Kid Ory, King Oliver, Sidney Bechet, and the young Louis Armstrong.

In 1917, Gertrude went on to form her own troupe. Billed as "Madame Gertrude Rainey and Her Georgia Smart Sets," the troupe consisted of Rainey backed by a chorus line of dancers and a five-piece band. The troupe, following up on Gertrude's already established reputation, caused an instant stir. Later, fronting a number of different bands, Rainey continued on as an enthusiastic entertainer, her whole lifetime being happily spent in music halls, theaters, and vaudeville tents. Her life could not have been spent any other way.

The ease with which Rainey moved through the sometimes chaotic world of show business can be misleading, though. It should not be forgotten that in Rainey's day, in black as well as white communities, women were not supposed to become performers. To do so meant flirting with extreme social disgrace. Among some African-Americans, the blues itself was thought to be "devil" music, as opposed to the "godly" hymns sung in church on Sundays. For a woman to embrace this sin-filled life was thought to be an

Ma Rainey's Jazz Band in 1925. The flamboyant
Rainey (1886–1939) was the consummate professional,
always delighting her audiences.

even worse fate than if a man became a blues musician. A man, went the common wisdom, was expected to wander a little, to mess around now and then, but a woman was always supposed to be "good." She was supposed to stay at home, marry a respectable fellow, raise a family, attend church socials, and be content with the joys and disappointments found in a thoroughly predictable, thoroughly domestic life.

Ma Rainey did none of these things. She left home, married a musician, and never raised a family. Although there is no evidence to suggest that her own family attempted to keep her from performing, Rainey nevertheless ran the double risk taken on by every black, professional female entertainer of the time. As an African-American, it was naturally assumed that she would be excluded from white society, but by becoming a performer Rainey also took the chance of being excluded from certain elements of black society as well. This was an act not for the faint of heart.

No one, though, would ever accuse Gertrude Rainey of being faint of heart. All who saw her were entranced by her extravagant, charismatic performances. She loved the attention, appearing onstage in a jewel-spangled, floor-length gown, waving an enormous ostrich-feather fan, and wearing a diamond-studded tiara crowning her elaborately curled wig. In performance Rainey let loose song after song—some funny, some mournful, some furious, some ecstatic. She carried the audience along with her, certain that with every laugh and nod of recognition she received, she was being given more and more proof that the audience was sitting delighted in the palm of her hand. When she took her bow and stepped back from the edge of the stage, the curtain sweeping shut in front of her, such a roar rose from the crowd that Rainey often went through one, two, three, four, five, six, seven curtain calls, until the show promoter, mopping his brow, had to turn on the lights and tell everyone to go home.

The fact was, Rainey and her audiences were in love with each other.

Rainey's talents went beyond performing. She was also a prolific songwriter and lyricist. Most singers—then, as now—did not write their own material, but of the ninety-two songs Rainey recorded, she either wrote or cowrote thirty-eight of them. With forty percent of her recorded repertoire to her own credit, Rainey was by far her own greatest source of music and lyrics.

Her greatest strength as a songwriter was her frank, realistic treatment of sexual subjects. Many of her songs deal with the wide varieties of relationships between men and women—men leaving their women, women leaving their men, men in love with women, women in love with men—in an unashamed, straightforward, and nonsensationalistic way that was rare in her time. For Rainey, sex was simply another aspect of life, one that, like anything else, could provide delight or despair, comfort or pain. In Rainey's songs there are no easy answers, no easy ways out. Her honest, down-to-earth approach to these subjects accounted in part for her deep and direct connection with her audiences. They knew that whatever she said, she wasn't lying.

Ma Rainey retired from the stage in 1935, at the age of forty-nine. She returned to Columbus and lived comfortably for four years until her death, even buying and managing two local theaters. In retirement she was no longer particularly well known—her fame having been eclipsed by that of Bessie Smith—but Rainey did not seem to care. She'd lived a rich, abundant life, according to her own rules. She was satisfied. That was enough. Fortunately for us, she'd paid close attention to that girl in the Missouri night, singing that strange and poignant song.

Bessie Smith

Bessie Smith was a volcano.

Her voice, her talent, her personality, her reputation: everything about Bessie Smith was as explosive, staggering, and fascinating as any vast venting of steam, rock, and ash.

And to this day, her shadow remains just as long as it did when she was alive. Despite all the singers who came before and after her, Bessie Smith, by the nature of her talent and the circumstances of her place and time, remains the quintessential blues singer.

Like Louis Armstrong, Smith was raised in poverty and was no stranger to "the blues." Shortly after her birth on April 25, 1894, in Chattanooga, Tennessee, her father died. By the time Bessie was in her teens, her mother and two of her brothers were dead as well. Bessie's oldest sister, Viola, became the head of this tattered household, and to do what she could to help her impoverished family, Bessie, still a child, began singing on street corners for spare change. This was, except for what she would observe from other singers later in her career, the sum total of her musical education—no lessons, no encouraging teachers, no adoring parents applauding at a recital. What Bessie Smith learned about music she learned on the streets of Chattanooga, singing at the top of her voice, holding out her hand, trying to grab the attention of anyone who passed.

Yet there must have been something about performing that appealed to Smith because by the age of eighteen she was hired on as a dancer in Moses Stoke's traveling minstrel group as it passed through Chattanooga. Smith's brother Clarence was already a member of the troupe, and—even more importantly—so was Ma Rainey.

There has been a great deal of speculation that Ma Rainey taught Smith how to sing, giving her instruction on technique and advice on choosing material. Although the two women were to become lifelong friends, no real evidence exists to suggest that Rainey took an active role in educating Smith about music. It's true that Smith could not have found a better role model, but for the most part whatever she learned came from close observation on Smith's part. As Rainey took her place in the center of the stage, spreading her arms toward an adoring audience, Smith—standing in a line of other dancers—no doubt looked on and was determined to become a star herself one day.

Although it was not long before she started singing on her own, Smith did not find success quickly or easily. She moved to Atlanta, toured the South and the East Coast on the T.O.B.A. circuit, and then moved to Philadelphia, where she performed regularly at the Standard and Dunbar theaters. As she traveled, Smith developed her own unique style. Making no attempt to sound "pretty," her voice was direct, forceful, sometimes growling and harsh. Likewise, her mannerisms were rough, and the gritty songs she chose to sing reflected her working-class background. She did not present herself as some kind of vulnerable, beautiful songbird: instead she was defiant, powerful, intolerant of fools.

Although this unusually rugged presence won her a following among black audiences who saw her in performance—and who no doubt identified with her passion—it was this same quality that initially prevented her from rising any farther in the music business. White recording executives found her voice and manner too coarse, and despite numerous attempts to gain a recording contract she was turned down again and again. One of the most remarkably wrongheaded evaluations of Smith's ability came from Thomas Alva Edison, famed inventor and founder of the world's first record company. Upon listening to Smith, Edison tersely jotted down, "Voice n.g. 4/21/24." Edison believed Smith's voice was simply "no good." Thus, Smith—later to be known as the "Empress of the Blues"—left Edison's offices without a contract. Stepping back onto the sidewalk once again, mulling over yet another rejection, Smith probably couldn't help but look back on her days singing on the streets of Chattanooga, wondering just how far she'd really come. Soon enough, though, a record company would come looking for her.

At this time, Columbia Records, a giant in the recording industry today, was near bankruptcy. Desperate for any kind of success, in need of quick cash, Columbia executives dispatched a man named Frank Walker to find new talent—as soon as possible. Walker had heard Smith perform in Selma, Alabama, back in 1917. He remembered Smith's strong performance, and, calculating that Columbia had virtually

This striking portrait of Bessie Smith (1894–1937) is not dated. Her first record, "Down Hearted Blues," became an instant hit and eventually made Smith popular with both black and white audiences.

nothing left to lose by approaching Smith, Walker offered her a contract. Smith agreed. Wary of record company executives, all of whom had so far given her nothing but grief, Smith went to Chicago to do the recording. There she laid down a number of tracks, and to the surprise of everyone her first record, "Down Hearted Blues," sold a dizzying 780,000 copies in the first six months of its release.

Up to this point, no single blues performer had so captured the public's imagination. Throughout the following decade Smith released hit after hit for Columbia, performing in cities where no blues singer had before, and as her popularity grew, crowds lined up around the block to buy her records and to see her in concert. She became popular with white as well as black audiences, but for blacks, Smith was something more than just a popular entertainer. She was a hero. Despite her wide popularity, she made no compromises in her singing style or selection of material: she remained direct, confrontational, truthful, passionate. She continued to present herself as she always had, as a strong black woman with something to say, and African-American audiences responded to her honesty and determination. She also continued to perfect her vocal ability: she learned to sing off the beat, to slur notes, to vary her style according to the demands of the song. This technical mastery, combined with her blazing presence, made her an incomparable performer. She enthralled audiences in city after city. Danny Barker, a jazz guitarist who saw her sing many times, described a Bessie Smith show this way:

> She could bring about mass hypnotism. When she was performing you could hear a pin drop. . . . When you went to see Bessie and she came out, that was it. If you had any church background, like people who came from the South, like I did, you would recognize a similarity between what she was doing and what those preachers and evangelists there did, and how they moved people. . . . Bessie did the same thing on stage.[3]

Perhaps it was Smith's sense of controlled anger that so affected, and continues to affect, her listeners. In her singing there is an unmistakable ongoing tension between her technique and her emotions. The strength of her emotions, like those of Robert Johnson, at times seems to threaten to overwhelm her musicianship; listening to her, you feel as though at any moment she might stop singing and just start screaming. Yet her work, however fraught with feeling, always remains art, never crosses the line into easy exhibitionism. As the song goes on, her singing gains greater and greater intensity, like a tightrope walker who is following a trembling line between art and violence, order and chaos. She gives us rage that is nevertheless controlled; control that is nevertheless filled with rage. Any young, aspiring artist, musical or otherwise, would be wise to learn this lesson from Smith.

An example of this aspect of Smith's art can be found in her lyrics to "Poor Man's Blues,"

> Mister rich man, rich man, open up your heart and mind,
> Mister rich man, rich man, open up your heart and mind,
> Give the poor man a chance, help stop these hard, hard times.
> When you're living in your mansion, you don't know what hard times mean,
> When you're living in your mansion, you don't know what hard times mean,
> Poor working man's wife is starving, your wife is living like a queen . . .
>
> Now the war is over, poor man must live the same as you,
> Now the war is over, poor man must live the same as you,
> If it wasn't for the poor man, mister rich man, what would you do?[4]

These lyrics are filled with pain and rage—and yet they are carefully written, each line creating a deeper and deeper impression on the listener. By combining passion and artistry, Smith delivers a withering vision of our world. It is no wonder that in segregated Jim Crow America, blacks looked to her as a champion: she was willing to speak the truth.

A myth surrounds the facts of Smith's death. On the morning of September 26, 1937, she was killed in an automobile accident on a road in rural Mississippi. Soon after, a rumor sprung up that she had died needlessly, more or less at the hands of a racist society. The story went that ambulance drivers had taken Smith to an all-white hospital, where, despite her obviously critical condition, she'd been refused admittance. Before the ambulance drivers had time to take her to a hospital that admitted blacks, Smith had bled to death.

Those who have closely investigated this story, however, have come to the conclusion that it was just that—a story, a fabrication. There appears to be no truth to this tale of ambulance drivers, white hospitals, and last-minute "what ifs." The rumor, though, does reveal a great deal about the impression Bessie Smith left behind. She seemed superhuman, not bound by the same laws as the rest of us, a woman so strong that she could be killed only by the most extraordinary measures. Surely, this rumor seems to say, Bessie Smith couldn't have died like anyone else; nothing as capricious as an automobile accident could have brought her down; nothing as simple as some unlucky twist of fate could have placed her in that car, on that road, on that day. Surely there had to be more to it than that.

She was human, though, subject to the same laws as the rest of us. But it's awfully hard to imagine a volcano disappearing so suddenly, just like that.

These were the early years of the blues—from its beginnings in the rural South to the stages around the world where Louis

Armstrong blew his trumpet. In purely chronological terms, we've covered the period of time lying roughly between 1900 and the late 1930s. Soon we'll pick up the thread of the story again, bringing it up to the present day.

In the meantime, though . . .

From the Top

So far, everything I've said is true. Robert Johnson can scare you half to death; Louis Armstrong revolutionized the role of the musical solo; people really did stand in block-long lines to see Bessie Smith. But all this overshadows at least one crucial point: the blues are, first and last, music. Everything accomplished by these artists was done through a conscious manipulation of scales, meters, chord progressions, and lyrics. These are the tools that Johnson, Armstrong, and Smith knew by heart. These are the elements they used in the pursuit of their craft. In this chapter, rather than looking at the people who created the blues, we'll look at the music itself.

So here's the bread and butter: the actual, basic stuff from which the blues are made.

To understand this chapter you'll have to be able to read music and to have access to some kind of instrument. I know that this might make things difficult for some readers—but I'm hoping this will encourage you to learn to read music and to get your hands on whatever instrument you can find. For readers who already can read music and who are already musicians, the material presented here will be very simple. Either way, no matter what your technical familiarity with music, the basics of the blues are so fundamental that everybody with an interest in music should be familiar with them.

Well, then.

One. Two. Three. Four . . .

The Blues Scale

In the key of C, the standard major scale of Western music looks like this:

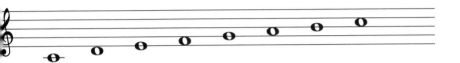

And the standard minor scale looks like this:

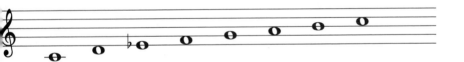

Although it's simplifying things a bit, you could say that the major scale sounds "happy," and the minor scale sounds "sad." These two scales are the basis of most European-based music, from Bach's fugues to Madonna's pop songs. In contrast, the blues scale is neither major nor minor. In the key of C, it looks like this:

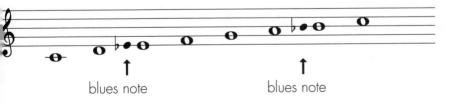

Obviously, the blues scale looks, and certainly sounds, different than the previous two scales. This is because early blues guitar players based their music in part upon African, rather than Western, scales. Not interested in playing in strict major or minor scales, these guitar players would often bend the strings of their guitars while they were playing. By bending these strings—and it's worth trying this out on a guitar yourself—the sound seemed to slide from note to note, rather than simply to move from separate note to separate note.

This is something that is impossible to do on a piano. On a piano you play individual notes and even when you hit two keys that sit right next to each other, there nevertheless remains a range of sound between the two notes that you cannot play. Thus, when the early blues players bent their strings, they were literally playing notes that had never been heard before—notes that, when you played the piano, were not even thought to exist. The standard methods for notating music, reflecting this belief, simply had no way of writing down these previously "nonexistent" notes.

The blues scales as shown on page 62, then, is in many ways not the true blues scale: it is just as near as one can get by transcribing the blues into standardized methods of notation. Nevertheless, over the years, this scale—used by blues piano players who could not bend their strings—has become accepted as being close enough to what these original guitar players had done.

What remains most important, however, is that this scale accurately captured the blues mood, the blues feeling. This was done by making a scale that was neither major nor minor and by including in the scale that came to be known as "blue" notes. These blue notes are those that approximate the sound of sliding between notes, as the early guitar players had done. In the example given above, these blue notes are E-flat and B-flat.

Chord Progressions

Although it is not true for many blues songs—and certainly not for the more musically complex elements of jazz that rose out

64

of the blues—the majority of blues songs follow a standard *chord progression*. A chord progression is simply a pattern of particular chords played in a particular order. So common is this particular progression to the blues, that it is more usually known as a blues progression. In the key of C, the blues progression looks like this:

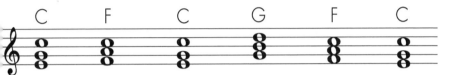

Regardless of what chord you start playing, on the piano the chords that follow are always five black and white keys, and then seven black and white keys, up from the original chord that you began with. So, for example, if you started with a B-flat instead of a C, the progression would look like this:

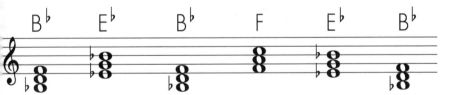

Again, this holds true for whatever chord you begin with. Start with a chord. Go five keys up. That's the next chord. Then go seven keys up. There's the final chord in the progression.

The basic blues chord progression is usually twelve measures long. That is, there are twelve measures of music consisting of four whole beats in each measure. In the key of C, the twelve-measure chord progression looks like this:

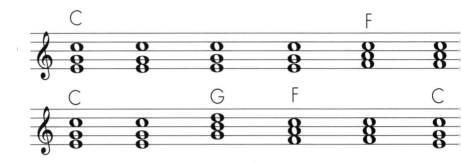

This pattern is also known as the *twelve-bar blues*.

Now, if we put these two elements together, the blues scale and the blues progression, we have all the basics of a blues song. We can do this by putting the chords in the bass clef and a scale-based melody in the treble clef, and we get something that looks like this:

And there you have it: a blues song. Nothing particularly original about it, but it does contain all the essentials, except for one—words.

Lyrics

When it comes to art, blues art or otherwise, it sometimes seems as if rules are made to be broken. For every piece of art that follows the rules, another doesn't. This is true for blues lyrics, as well. Most blues lyrics follow a certain pattern, a certain set of rules, but there are many that do not. For our purposes, though, we'll examine the standard pattern, keeping in mind that this is certainly not the only way to write a blues lyric.

Most blues lyrics follow what has come to be known as the AAB pattern. This means that the first phrase is repeated before the second phrase is introduced. To understand this better, let's look at an example, taken from the traditional folk song "I Know You, Rider."

> *I know you, rider,*
> *   gonna miss me when I'm gone.*
> *I know you, rider,*
> *   gonna miss me when I'm gone.*
> *Gonna miss your baby from rollin' in your arms.*

In this example, the phrase "I know you, rider, gonna miss me when I'm gone" is repeated before the next phrase, "Gonna miss your baby from rollin' in your arms," is introduced. If we attach the letter A to this first phrase, and the letter B to the second, we get this:

> *A   I know you, rider,*
> *   gonna miss me when I'm gone.*
> *A   I know you, rider,*
> *   gonna miss me when I'm gone.*
> *B   Gonna miss your baby from*
> *   rollin' in your arms.*

Thus we have the classic AAB blues lyric pattern. With all the lyrics in front of us, we can see how this AAB pattern is maintained in each stanza, throughout the whole song.

I know you, rider,
    gonna miss me when I'm gone.
I know you, rider,
    gonna miss me when I'm gone.
Gonna miss your baby from rollin' in your arms.

Laid down last night,
    lord I could not take my rest.
Laid down last night,
    lord I could not take my rest.
My mind was wanderin' with the
    wild geese in the West.

Oh the sun's gonna shine
    in my back door some day.
Oh the sun's gonna shine
    in my back door some day.
And the wind will blow all my troubles away.

I wish I was a headlight
    on a northbound train.
I wish I was a headlight
    on a northbound train.
I'd shine my light through the cool Colorado rain.

I know you, rider,
    gonna miss me when I'm gone.
I know you, rider,
    gonna miss me when I'm gone.
Gonna miss your baby from rollin' in your arms.

Again, not every blues lyric follows this pattern, but most do. One reason for this might lie in the fact that most early blues were improvised, meaning that the singers simply made up the song and the words as they went. Repeating the first phrase gave thinking-on-their-feet performers a little extra time to think of a word that would rhyme with the last word of the phrase. So, in "I Know You, Rider," we get "gone/arms," "rest/West," "day/away," and "train/rain," which probably came from someone who was working under pressure to think up instantaneous rhymes. In this way, these blues lyrics are similar to improvised raps, in which the rapper riffs off a string of seemingly spontaneous rhymes, to the amazement of his or her listeners.

Another interesting aspect of blues lyrics is that they entirely dispense with the usual pattern known as "verse/chorus." In this pattern, which is followed by most popular songs, today as much as ever, the lyrics go back and forth between introducing new phrases (or "the verse") and repeating throughout the song one unchanging phrase, or "the chorus." Likewise, the music to the verse is different from that of the chorus. Although the blues lyrics may indeed repeat words or phrases, they rarely return to such a musically and lyrically definite chorus.

With all this in mind, let's go back to the music we wrote, this time adding a title and a few words.

House on Fire Blues

Spoken: House on fire . . .   Don't know what to do . . .   House on fire, baby . . .

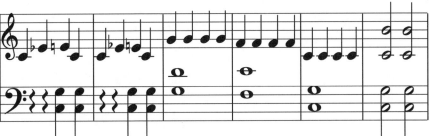

Don't know what to do. . .   Watch me jump outa window, baby. . .   Fall right on you.

And there it is, a complete blues song. There's nothing spectacular about it, either in its music or its lyrics, and any professional blues player would elaborate upon its simplicity. That's not the point, though. The point is, that these, pure and simple, are the essential elements of the blues. Without them, there would be no blues at all.

The Middle Years

*T*he Great Depression of the 1930s hit the blues audience hard. With banks shutting down, farms foreclosing, and jobs being more and more difficult to find, who had the money to buy records, attend concerts, or pay admission to traveling vaudeville shows? Although in the late 1920s, because of the popularity of such performers as Bessie Smith, the blues had begun to cross racial lines, it had not yet crossed class boundaries. Most of the blues audience was poor to begin with, and in this time of grinding economic hardship, this audience saw its buying power all but vanish. As a result, recording companies went out of business, contracts were allowed to lapse, and no new performers were hired. The boom that had sent record companies' scouts scrambling throughout the South to find every blues musician that might make a buck or two was over.

Yet, hard times were nothing new to the blues. The blues, as we've seen, rose out of painful and even desperate social conditions. It had never been easy, and now not only was the whole United States in financial trouble, but for blacks all the policies and indignities of segregation remained firmly in place, stacking difficulty upon difficulty. Despite the continuing efforts of socially conscious lawyers, union organizers, writers, and everyday people, the civil rights movement was still some twenty years away. Nevertheless, thanks to the artists found in this chapter, the blues did indeed survive the Great Depression. They not only survived but matured, so that by the 1960s they had reached an unprecedented, worldwide popularity.

Individuals might come and go, but the blues come from a place in the heart that is so true that they are bigger than any individual or event. In that sense, you can throw a depression, or segregation, or anything you like at the blues, and they'll always get up and start walking again.

Huddie "Leadbelly" Ledbetter

In many ways, Huddie Ledbetter, now known almost exclusively by the nickname of Leadbelly, was one of the first generation of blues musicians. In Texas and Louisiana, between 1905 and 1917, he played with the infamous Blind Lemon Jefferson. But it was not until many years later, in 1935, in the midst of the Great Depression, that he came to be known outside of the relatively small circle of people who'd heard him play in those Southern towns. This isn't to say that Leadbelly hadn't been busy in the intervening years. According to Leadbelly, no doubt, he'd been all too busy, involved in matters he'd rather have never known anything about: prison, for example.

A man of great physical strength, hence the name Leadbelly, Huddie Ledbetter was born in January 1888 on the Louisiana side of the Texas-Louisiana border. His father and mother, Wes and Sallie, were sharecroppers who worked hard to own their own farmland. With Huddie helping out, plowing, planting, and picking cotton almost every day of his life, they were finally able to buy some seventy acres. Huddie's strength was a great asset to the family: Wes and Sallie had four other children, but none of them survived childhood. On a cotton farm, your only hope of getting ahead was by sheer will and strength of character, and Huddie seemed gifted with more character and will than one could

Huddie "Leadbelly" Ledbetter (1885–1949) performs for
a group of school children in the 1940s.

ever ask for. It was almost as if he was making up for the work that would have been done by the brothers and sisters he never knew. According to neighbors, Huddie and his father could pick more cotton in a shorter amount of time than anyone else in the county.

Although no one had probably ever gone at a plow with more passion than Huddie, he was even more passionate about music. At seven he was already picking out songs on a small accordian given to him by an uncle, and at school he became the guitar and mandolin player in a four-person band. Likewise, while he was working in the fields he often sang to himself, and he played organ for the nearby church he and his parents attended.

Music seemed to flow through him. Like so many early blues musicians, he had little formal musical training, but this made no difference to Huddie. He was a natural. While he was still a young man, he began to play guitar at weekly country dances, known as sooky jumps, where he proved himself to be a flamboyant and well-liked entertainer. He told tall tales along with his songs, acting out the lyrics as if they were lines from a play; his clear, powerful, trumpetlike voice instantly grabbed the attention of anyone close enough to hear.

Growing in confidence and skill, Huddie traveled to Shreveport, Louisiana, where he played to equal enthusiasm in the taverns of Fannin Street, the main thoroughfare through the black part of town. No doubt Huddie's fierce and fiery personality was coming through plain and clear in these performances. Along with his obvious musical ability, his natural charisma made him renowned throughout Shreveport. Yet it was this same volatile personality that got Huddie Ledbetter into trouble again and again throughout his life.

After returning home from playing one of his tours with Blind Lemon Jefferson, Ledbetter had his first encounter with the law. Precisely what the circumstances were, no one knows for sure. According to some accounts, Ledbetter got into a fistfight over a woman; others claim that he was arrested for waving a gun around. Given Huddie's temperament, either—or any one of another dozen accounts—might be true. Yet whatever led to it, on September 8, 1915, he was sentenced to thirty days in the Harrison County Jail. As payment to the lawyer they'd hired to defend Huddie, his parents had to sign over their land. At the stroke of a pen, the farm they'd worked for all their lives was gone, now in the hands of the lawyers who'd failed to get their son acquitted. And Huddie was left swinging a pick on the Harrison County road gang.

That didn't last long. Whatever obstacle Ledbetter found in his path, he felt it could be conquered by his own stubbornness and strength. Three days into his sentence, he lifted the chains from around his legs and ran across a field, fleeing the chain gang. Guards shouted at him, sent their dogs after him, and fired their rifles at him, but Huddie made it into some nearby woods. With the guards close behind, he persuaded some farmhands he passed to split his chains with an axe, and he threw the dogs off his trail by running down the middle of a stream. He'd made it. He was free again.

No one knew where to find him, and soon the hunt was over for Leadbelly.

But it seemed that a pattern had been set. Although he returned to playing his music—he went back on the road with Blind Lemon Jefferson—it was not long before he was in trouble again, this time with even more serious consequences.

On the night of December 13, 1917, Huddie and three acquaintances—Ellic Griffen, Will Stafford, and Lee Brown—were walking along a dark dirt road in Texas, on their way to a dance. Somewhere along the way a fight broke out between the four men. Words were said, punches thrown, and before anyone knew what had happened, Stafford lay dead in the middle of the road, shot in the chest. Months later, on April 22, 1918, Ledbetter—the only one of the four who had a gun—was convicted of killing Stafford. Did he shoot Stafford? Or was Leadbelly to be believed when he insisted to the court that the other two men overpowered him, took his gun, and shot Stafford? Perhaps the jury was correct in convicting him, and perhaps it was not. In any case, Huddie received a sentence of a minimum of seven years and a maximum of thirty years, to be served in the Texas State Prison.

And still the pattern continued: this time, after serving three years of his sentence, he tried to escape. He was not to be lucky twice. He was caught and returned to prison, a place he'd come to hate more than death.

A black prison in the South in the first half of this century was an institution of almost unimaginable cruelty. Most were nothing more than enormous cotton plantations. Beneath the blazing hot sun, under the watchful eyes of guards on horses with rifles at the ready, the prisoners were led to the fields, where they worked from sunrise to sunset every day of the year. Prisoners were sometimes summarily shot or beaten to death for the slightest infraction of prison rules, such as not showing proper "respect" to guards. Often the only thing separating the prisoners from the other, nearby "free" plantations was a high barbed-wire fence through which the prisoners could look and see other African-Americans, stooped over the cotton stalks just like they were, hacking at the dirt just like they were. With very little imagination at all it could seem that for any black, anywhere in the South, the whole world was one gigantic prison.

Remarkably—or perhaps not so remarkably, given the long African-American tradition of dealing with physical and psychological pain through music—various forms of songwriting and playing flourished inside the prisons. Like their slave ancestors, the prisoners frequently sang songs to coordinate with their grueling work. Because music was one of the only forms of entertainment available to the prisoners, many became skilled musicians in an attempt to create, through their playing and singing, a more meaningful world than the one in which they had wound up. Regardless of whatever brutal social circumstances gave rise to these songs, and whatever psychological purposes they might have served, the songs invented and performed by the prisoners were often of first-rate artistic quality. One reason for this high quality was those professional musicians who found themselves picking cotton behind that barbed-wire fence. One of these was Leadbelly.

So proficient were a number of these prison musicians that many influential whites made special trips to the prisons, just to hear them play and sing. After all, the music was good, and there was never an admission price. Among these influential visitors was the governor of Texas, Pat Neff. Like the king of some bizarre court, Neff would arrive at the prison, seat himself on a porch, and, flanked by guards, sip whiskey in the evening light and listen to the prison musicians as they were paraded in front of him. The prison was, more or less, Neff's private music hall.

He had never, though, seen a performer in this orchestra quite like Leadbelly.

Upon hearing that Neff was planning a visit, Leadbelly composed a song especially for the occasion: one in which he would boldly plead to the governor for a pardon. Neff was taken by the song and Leadbelly's ability, promising to take his case under consideration. Neff came back to the prison a number of times, and Leadbelly continued to perform for him; yet months passed with no mention of release. And then the word came: in one of his last acts as governor, Neff had pardoned Leadbelly, who was four months away from serving the minimum sentence.

So Leadbelly was free to pursue his music again. He moved back to Shreveport, to pick up where he had left off. But his freedom was not to last long. The pattern still held.

On January 15, 1930, Huddie was in downtown Shreveport. A Salvation Army band passed by, marching down the street, playing "Onward, Christian Soldiers." Huddie, enjoying the song, tapped his feet along with it—so that he almost seemed to be dancing. According to Blanche Love, one of Leadbelly's cousins, a nearby group of whites thought his behavior inappropriate and "irreligious." They told him to quit dancing and to move along. He moved along, but some distance down the street he began dancing again. Outraged by the "insolence" of this black man, the crowd surrounded him, demanding that he stop. Now it was no longer simply a matter of Huddie's not showing enough respect to the Salvation Army band: by continuing to dance, despite "orders" to the contrary, he was directly challenging white authority. Leadbelly, who had no doubt seen more trouble in his life than those in the crowd could even imagine, was too proud to do anyone else's bidding, and he told the crowd that he would not stop. He insisted he had a right to dance whenever, wherever he wanted. Knives were drawn. Leadbelly drew his knife and wounded one of the whites. The police arrived. The white man was taken to the hospital, and Leadbelly, who suffered a gash to his head, was taken to jail.

That night word flew around Shreveport that a "drunk-crazed Negro" had attacked a white man. A mob formed, intent upon lynching the "attacker." They stormed the jail, ready to drag Leadbelly into the streets and kill him. Fortunately, the police held the crowd at bay, and when word was received that the white man would recover from his wounds, the lynch mob dispersed.

Yet the message from the crowd was clear: it might be one thing for Leadbelly to get into a fight with, or even kill, another black man. It was another thing entirely to cut a white man's arm.

Five weeks later, on February 25, 1930, Leadbelly was sentenced to a term of no less than six and no more than eight years for attempted murder, to be served in the Louisiana State Penitentiary.

It's hard to determine what effect these traumatic events had upon Leadbelly. He was forty-two years old and faced the prospect of spending yet another seeming lifetime in another prison, this time for a crime he committed in self-defense. Yet he did not try to escape the penitentiary. Instead, he made himself into a model prisoner, all the while petitioning the governor of Louisiana, O. K. Allen, for a pardon. Years passed. Leadbelly continued living the soul-destroying prison life, all the while remaining the perfect inmate and seeking out every possible legal means of getting himself out. He'd already spent too many years behind those barbed-wire fences. His life was passing before him.

At this time folklorist John Lomax and his son, Alan, were traveling through the South, collecting and recording African-American prison songs. Lomax was one of the first white intellectuals to recognize the artistry to be found in black folk songs. Working for the Library of Congress, with a primitive record-making mechanism installed in the trunk of his car, he was gathering all the examples of this oft-overlooked music that he could find. By chance, the Lomaxes stopped at the state prison at Angola, Louisiana, where Leadbelly was serving his sentence.

Upon hearing Leadbelly, Lomax realized that he was a musician of nearly unparalleled stature, and legend has it that Lomax petitioned for, and secured, Leadbelly's pardon. This was not the case, however. The years of good behavior, the questionable nature of the sentence itself, and Leadbelly's continuing efforts to obtain a pardon on his own behalf, all combined to convince the governor to commute Leadbelly's sentence.

Nevertheless, his connection with the Lomaxes proved worthwhile. Initially, Leadbelly became their chauffeur as they continued to travel through the South. Then, with their support, Leadbelly moved to New York City, where he began his musical career once again with a series of performances. Leadbelly caused a sensation in New York. Playing for mostly white audiences who had probably never heard anything quite like Leadbelly's music, he struck a deep chord in those who saw him play. The country at the time was still mired in the depression: Leadbelly's songs of economic hardship and social injustice now spoke to a wider number of people than ever before, all of whom by now had seen some hard times of their own.

In New York, Leadbelly was soon joined by white folk-singers such as Woody Guthrie and Pete Seeger. He also began to release a series of recordings, among them songs such as as "Goodnight, Irene," "Midnight Special," and "Rock Island Line," all of which have now become standards of American popular music. In the last years of his life Leadbelly developed amyotrophic lateral sclerosis, or Lou Gehrig's disease. Much to his embarrassment, the disease had robbed him of much of his muscular stamina. Pete Seeger recalls playing a concert with Leadbelly, and how he struggled to continue playing.

He was deeply ashamed that his strength had left. He didn't want to be seen walking onto stage with a cane. He said, "Let me walk on stage, I'll sit down, then you open the curtain for me. Okay?" After the performance, they closed the curtain on him, then with pain he'd get his cane and leave the stage.[1]

Leadbelly was proud to the end. The man who had fled across a field from prison guards did not want to be seen exiting life, needing help, holding a cane. He died in New York City on December 6, 1949.

Because of the sheer fireworks of Leadbelly's life—his multiple incarcerations and escapes, his fate so often lying in the hands of those who cared nothing for him, his indefatigable spirit helping him start life over and over again—it is all too easy to overlook the quality of Leadbelly's work and to miss the enormous musical influence he had upon those around him. Bob Dylan, another American master, has frequently acknowledged his debt to Leadbelly, and it was the impression Leadbelly left upon New York audiences that, in large part, sparked what eventually came to be known as the "blues revival" of the 1960s (which will be discussed later in this chapter). The fact remains that no other single blues musician has ever achieved the vast popularity of Leadbelly. More than forty-five years after his death, his songs can still be found in record stores, school songbooks, and hymnals. If I have concentrated more upon Leadbelly's life than his music, it is only because of the limits of space and the particularly emblematic nature of his life in relation to the development of the blues. An equally long and detailed discussion of the purely musical aspects of Leadbelly's work could easily be written.

Billie Holiday

A cloud of self-destructive romance surrounds Billie Holiday. To many she is the quintessential blues singer: a woman of celestial talent who has suffered celestial pain, standing alone in a spotlight in smoky nightclubs, delivering moving songs of heartache. To others, particularly some jazz and blues critics, her reputation is hopelessly overblown; one commentator observed that some critics deemed her songs and style "the pathetic sound of an attractive but wretched woman crying in self-pity."[2]

So which is it?

Both of these evaluations are based more on Holiday's life than her art. Like Huddie Ledbetter, Holiday lived a dramatic, volatile, even tragic life. The stories about her upbringing, her promiscuity, her drug addiction, will, depending on your preference, make her all the more attractive or all the more pitiful. Much of this differing opinion is based upon the enormously popular but factually incorrect book of Holiday's life called *Lady Sings the Blues.* (The movie of the same name, in typical Hollywood style, only served to perpetuate the book's myths.) Written by William Dufty in collaboration with Holiday, the book is little more than a publicity stunt on both their parts, and whatever information is given there should be viewed with some degree of skepticism.

Regardless of what is written here, the debate will go on concerning Holiday's music, her character, and the relationship between the two. Yet everyone agrees that Holiday, whatever opinion you hold of her, certainly deserves attention. So what do the facts say about Holiday?

They add up to reveal a virtuoso artist and a desperately unhappy person.

As with so many blues musicians, our understanding of Holiday's early life is made up of much speculation. According to Holiday, she was born in Baltimore, Maryland, on April 17, 1915. Most blues scholars, however, believe that she was probably three years older.[3] Likewise, other stories of her early life—that she was physically beaten by relatives, that she was forced to work in a brothel, that as a teenager she spent four months in jail—are probably partly true. It is obvious, however, that Holiday had nothing resembling a happy childhood. She was raised in poverty, and her father, Clarence Holiday, refused to recognize her as his own child until she had become famous—and then he was eager to claim credit for her success.

Around 1930, though, the real story of her life becomes a little more clear. It was at this time that she began working

Billie Holiday (1915–57)

as a singer in New York clubs, and after some three years of working off and on, she got her first big break. She was singing at Monette's Supper Club, on 133rd Street in Harlem, when she was heard by that omnipresent blues and jazz promoter John Hammond. (It was Hammond who, five years later, was to put on the *From Spirituals to Swing* show at Carnegie Hall, which was supposed to have featured Robert Johnson.) Hammond was rightfully impressed with Holiday, and within months, he arranged a recording of Holiday singing with Benny Goodman's band. Also about this time, Holiday began getting more prestigious bookings, playing, among other places, the legendary Apollo Theater on 125th Street.

Initially, Holiday was considered to have limited commercial appeal. This was mainly because of her thoroughly inventive and distinct vocal style. Unlike her predecessors, such as Ma Rainey and Bessie Smith, Holiday did not have a large, full, expansive voice. In contrast, Holiday's voice was small and controlled, with a slightly nasal quality, almost like that of a trumpet with a mute placed in its bell. In fact, Holiday based her vocal style on Louis Armstrong's trumpet playing. She frequently mentioned that when she was singing, she felt like she was playing a horn. One of the most remarkable aspects of Holiday's skill was the way in which, like Armstrong, she was able to improvise around a melody. She could stretch it out so that she was often singing off the straight beat, adding an emotional tension to her music that was missing in that of other singers who, lacking her skill, never varied from the established melody and rhythm. Likewise, she injected plainly dissonant notes into her singing, letting them hang in the air, adding yet another passionate effect to her music, one that mirrored the sense of pain and conflict often found in her lyrics. Of all the singers of her time, Holiday was probably the single most original and conscientious musician, crafting her art with absolutely deliberate intent.

One of the most interesting elements of Holiday's style was that despite her careful approach, her songs often sound wonderfully casual and spontaneous. Rather than trying to fill essentially easygoing love songs with false importance

83

and emotion, Holiday kept it simple, relaxed, and thus fun and believable. (Most pop singers today have not learned from Holiday's example. Singers performing love songs on MTV or VH-1 almost invariably deliver their songs in an overblown, unbelievably serious manner, making the clichéd lyrics sound all the more ridiculous.) Holiday's delightful number "Them There Eyes," for example, is a bit of romantic fluff. It is not meant to change the world, nor is it meant to say anything especially profound. By treating her material this way, Holiday makes the music more engaging. As an artist, she knew how to match her delivery to the seriousness or lightheartedness of her material. Ironically, Holiday's frequently offhand, charming manner is in direct contrast to the criticism that her music was overdramatic and self-pitying.

This is not to say that Holiday restricted herself to essentially lightweight work. One of her most well-known songs, for example, is "Strange Fruit," which describes in graphic, bloody detail the appearance of a black corpse hanging from a tree, following a lynching in the American South. I remember the first time I ever heard Holiday's version of this song. Appropriately enough, I was driving down a dark country road, and the words and music coming from the radio were so direct and disturbing that I pulled to the side of the road, wanting to pay absolute attention to the song, no longer caring where I was going. In calmer retrospect, what is probably most startling about Holiday's rendition of "Strange Fruit" is that despite the blatantly horrific nature of the song, her singing remains as restrained, as clipped, and as lilting as ever. She in fact delivers the words "burning flesh" with such delicacy that you would think she was asking a lover for a kiss. Needless to say, the effect is disorienting, frightening, and altogether dizzying.

It also required a great deal of courage on Holiday's part to sing such a truthful song in public.

Eventually, audiences became used to Holiday's new style of singing, and she went on to gain a genuine degree of national popularity. Although she did not reach the household status of other contemporary singers, such as Kate Smith or

Bing Crosby—and it is unlikely that, given the time, any African-American man or woman could have done so—she became a well-known, highly paid performer.

Unfortunately, she was not able to enjoy what she had worked so hard to achieve. In fact, the more success she had, the more turbulent her life became. At some point in 1942, she began using heroin, and soon, despite her claims to the contrary, she was addicted. Complicating this situation, she had a string of disastrous relationships with men, who were also usually addicts and who saw in Holiday a way of getting rich. They frequently manipulated her and begged for money; one framed her for his drug possession charge. Between addiction, inattention to business matters, and the abusive relationships she maintained, she was perpetually broke. From 1942 until her death in July 1959, she seemed to be on a slow and relentless slide: she was arrested on more drug charges, began drinking heavily, smoked some fifty cigarettes a day, and frequently in performance was so weak that audiences weren't always sure she would make it through a song. Not surprisingly, the quality of her work suffered. Relatively few of her performances or recordings matched those she had done at the beginning of her career.

Eventually the years of self-abuse took their toll. On the afternoon of May 31, 1959, she collapsed into a coma. She was treated for ten weeks at the Metropolitan Hospital in New York, where detectives repeatedly searched her room for narcotics. They found nothing. She finally died of complications arising from cirrhosis, a liver disease, and was buried at St. Raymond's Cemetery in the Bronx.

What had happened? How could she have fallen so far?

Almost everyone has a theory to explain her decline. Some say it was her childhood. Some believe that it was the social pressures of the times. Others blame it on the record industry, and still others fault Holiday herself. More than likely, her demise was a result of all these factors. But this much seems clear: despite her enormous talent, Billie Holiday doubted herself all her life. She was tremendously sensitive to audiences' reactions, and she feared being abandoned, even by those who mistreated her. She lacked a core belief in herself that would have allowed her to cope with fame, as her idol Louis Armstrong had done. Was this because her father abandoned her early in life? Or because of the confining roles assigned to women of the time? Or something else entirely? We'll never really know, and it's likely that Holiday never knew, either. At the end she was sad, lonely, lost, and tired.

Holiday's artistry should be a model to everyone, her life a model to no one.

McKinley "Muddy Waters" Morganfield

In comparison to Huddie Ledbetter and Billie Holiday, McKinley Morganfield, better known as Muddy Waters, lived a stable and fairly conventional, if not always easy, life. He is proof that you do not have to mire yourself in destructiveness to be a successful artist. Along with Louis Armstrong, Muddy Waters was the most influential blues player who ever lived. If you ask someone to describe what the blues sound like, more than likely he or she will describe that brand of music perfected in Chicago, between 1945 and 1950, by Muddy Waters and his band.

He was born on April 4, 1915, in Rolling Fork, Mississippi. For a future bluesman, he could not have come into the world in a better time or in a better place. This was the heart of Mississippi Delta country, the cradle of the blues, home to such luminaries as Charley Patton, Son House, and Robert Johnson. In fact, we now pick up that thread of the blues story that we left with Robert Johnson. Johnson's principal teacher had been Son House, who in turn had learned to play from Charley Patton. Son House also taught young Muddy Waters how to play. Thus, a direct line of blues guitar lineage can be traced from Charley Patton to Son House to Robert Johnson and Muddy Waters. This heritage could not have fallen into more deserving or skillful hands: from this inherited wealth of musical knowledge, Waters would create something uniquely and impressively his own.

Muddy Waters (1915–83) sets the house on fire, playing his guitar and singing the blues. By incorporating the electric guitar and a 4/4 beat into his music, Waters created a new style of blues that influenced countless rock and blues musicians.

As a young man Waters was uncertain of his talent. He made his living working as a field hand, and on the side he ran a small juke joint where he sold his homemade whiskey and played guitar on the weekends. As for becoming a professional musician, Muddy felt that this was a fate belonging only to those prestigious players, like Patton and House, who had preceded him. Muddy was essentially a shy and quiet man. For the first twenty-six years of his life, he had never traveled more than a hundred miles from where he'd been born; and the world where these earlier bluesmen had ventured, played, and found success seemed an utterly strange and foreign place. In his life, Waters had seen little more than dusty back roads and sweltering cotton fields. Thus it's not surprising that the thought of becoming an entertainer on the same level with these great performers probably seemed no more than a dream to Waters.

He changed his mind, however, on an extraordinary afternoon in July 1941. It was at this time that Alan Lomax, continuing his father's undertaking, was once again traveling the South, collecting the music of rural African-Americans. Just as his dad had done, Lomax was working out of Washington, D.C., for the Library of Congress, and he'd brought with him a bulky recording apparatus that cut crude vinyl discs, which could immediately be played back on a record player. As he crisscrossed Coahoma County in northwestern Mississippi, Lomax was told again and again that he should get in touch with a guitarist and singer named Muddy Waters. One day, after some searching, Lomax found him at the end of a narrow dirt road, where Waters was working at his juke joint. Lomax explained that he was making a series of recordings, that he had been given Muddy's name, and that he was hoping he could record him as well. Waters agreed, but, ironically, he had just loaned his guitar to a friend. Fortunately, Lomax had a guitar with him—and by the time the recording session was over, both men were astounded. As he sat and listened to what Waters had done, Lomax felt that Waters's playing obviously went "right beyond all his predecessors." Waters, more humbly, heard his own voice issuing from the speaker on the record player, and said to himself, in astonishment, "I can *do* it. I can *do* it."[4]

Listening to his work on record gave Waters the distance he needed to realize that he was just as good as any other blues musician—maybe even better. After Lomax returned to Washington, he sent a copy of the recordings to Waters, and Waters, proud of what he'd done, promptly put them on juke-boxes in nearby Clarksdale. Everyone who heard the records was struck by their quality, and many encouraged Muddy to pursue his music. Finally, after much deliberation, Waters decided to act. He had become convinced that he had talent, and that he did not have much of a future staying in the South, working for low farm wages. In the most momentous choice of his life, Waters decided to move north to Chicago to what for him must have seemed the very edge of the earth, where jobs were more plentiful and where there was a burgeoning music scene. On a Friday morning, he sent word to the farm boss that he was sick. He packed his few belongings and later that afternoon he caught the Illinois Central out of Clarksdale, heading north.

In the first half of this century, many African-Americans had made the same choice as Waters. Following World War I, a literal exodus of black Americans had begun, leaving the South for the industrialized cities of the North—Chicago, in particular. Like Waters, they were seeking greater freedom and opportunity, hoping to escape the oppressive sharecropper system. By the time of World War II, this exodus had become a flood. Between 1940 and 1950, an estimated 154,000 blacks arrived in Chicago from the South, a number large enough to constitute a good-sized city. Considering that Chicago was already a sprawling metropolis, this sudden and constant influx of residents made the city feel as if it was nearly bursting at the seams. There were too many people and not enough space. In tenement row after tenement row, black migrants slept four, five, six to a room. Demand for a place to live was so great that landlords could charge whatever price they wished, knowing that if one tenant did not take a room, someone else would.

The city that had attracted these black migrants was not a particularly hospitable place: in the plain words of blues writer Robert Palmer, Chicago was "cold, expensive, dirty, and dangerous."[5]

But Chicago did have the one thing that everyone needed—jobs. Shortly after arriving there, after getting a little more used to the rushing cars, crowded sidewalks, and brick and steel canyons of a big city, Waters found work in a container factory. During the next few years he would hold a number of jobs, such as driving a delivery truck, but making music remained his goal and passion. And soon he would get his hands on the instrument with which he would transform the blues.

This was the electric guitar.

The invention of the electric guitar is another one of those moments in American music that remains clouded by legend. Guitarist Les Paul is generally given credit for refining, and sometimes for inventing, this now-common instrument. But no one knows for sure who first hooked a resonating magnet to a guitar and then ran the resulting sound through an electric amplifier. Likewise, it is impossible to say who was the first electric blues guitarist. Arthur "Big Boy" Crudup, another Mississippi native who moved to Chicago, was known to have played the blues on an electric guitar as early as 1939, a full two years before Waters was first contacted by Lomax. (Interestingly enough, it was Crudup who also recorded the original version of a song called "That's All Right": a song that Elvis Presley would later copy almost note for note in his own first commercial recording.) Yet regardless of who was first, it was Muddy Waters who truly revolutionized the blues through the use of the electric guitar.

The sound Waters developed was wholly his own. As if reflecting the harsh, urban environment where it was born, and in apparent contrast to his reserved personality, Waters's slide sound was fierce, searing, aggressive. By turning up his amplifier to the point where its vacuum tubes were overheating, Waters created such effects as distortion and feedback, techniques that are now so common they seem to have always existed. In fact, it was Waters who turned what most guitarists of his time would have considered mistakes into these infinitely expressive and widely copied methods. By playing with his band at such Chicago nightspots as the Du Drop Lounge and the Flame Club, and through a number of personnel changes and musical experiments, Waters was putting the finishing touches on his thunderous style.

Another crucial element of Waters's sound came through his standardization of blues rhythm into common 4/4 time. Up until this time, the majority of Mississippi blues guitarists—such as Patton, House, and Johnson—had all played solo, accomp-anying themselves as they sang. There had been no need to establish rhythms that a number of musicians could follow. For example, Johnson's rhythmic sense was very idiosyncratic, the speed of his playing often varying within a song, depending on how he wished to play at the moment. While this added an exhilarating tension and spontaneity to Johnson's music, it would have been all but impossible for a band to anticipate and play along with these sudden changes. Waters, however, in his pursuit of a bigger and more powerful sound, wanted to be backed up by a group of musicians. To accomplish this, he needed to establish a regular, steady beat in his music, so that others could play along with him. Interestingly, the beat that seemed to work best was common 4/4 time. This four-beat-per-measure rhythm was familiar to all the musicians who played with Waters, and though it was simple, it possessed the heavy driving force Waters sought.

These two changes, the incorporation of the electric guitar and the use of the 4/4 beat, gave the blues an utter-ly new sound. This style would eventually be defined as the "urban blues," or in Waters's words, the "deep blues." By now, Waters had decided that more people than those visiting the Chicago clubs needed to hear this new sound. Again, Waters's seemingly placid personality was in apparent contrast to his ambitions: he was determined to make his music nationally known, and he methodically set about to achieve this goal.

Waters was helped enormously by the success of his early recordings. The first popular record showcasing his signature sound was a single put out by the now-famous Chess Records label. It featured the songs "I Can't Be Satisfied" and "Feel Like Going Home." Although "I Can't Be Satisfied" is probably the stronger of the two songs, the title of "Feel Like Going Home" speaks volumes in terms of blues history. In a sense, "going home" was partly what Waters was doing with his music: although his sound was new, with its electric guitars and 4/4 beat, in other ways it was still based on the old Mississippi Delta style he'd learned as a boy. Or perhaps more accurately, by fusing these influences he was bringing his home north to the recording studios of Chicago, where it was to grow to worldwide proportions.

It is impossible to overstate the influence Waters had on other musicians of the time, both those who played the blues and those who did not. Waters continued to release records, frequently featuring songs written by his collaborator, Willie Dixon; he secured bona fide hits with such songs as "Hootchie Cootchie Man" and "They Call Me Muddy Waters"; he toured throughout the United States; and in 1958, in perhaps the single most influential musical tour of all time, he played a string of dates in England. Although other American blues musicians, such as Big Bill Broonzy and Billie Holiday, had already appeared in Europe, no one had played the blues with such intensity, and at sometimes deafening volume, as Waters. The English papers raved about him. Aspiring musicians crowded against the stage, hanging on his every move, trying to remember every note he played. Record collectors hustled to get whatever Waters had released on vinyl. Among those who Waters impressed were five Englishmen, barely out of their teens, whose names would later become household words: John Lennon, Paul McCartney, Mick Jagger, Keith Richard, and Eric Clapton. Jagger and Richard even went so far as to name their band "The Rolling Stones," after a phrase Waters had sung to John Lomax on what now seemed to be that far-away afternoon, back in a cabin at the end of a dirt road, down in Mississippi.

Willie Dixon (1915–83)—producer, composer, bassist, and singer—wrote many blues standards, including "I'm Your Hoochie Coochie Man" and "Built for Comfort."

Unlike Holiday, Waters was able to handle the success and fame that now came to him; and unlike Leadbelly, he did not have the mercurial temperament that otherwise could have undermined his career. Instead, Waters continued to work steadily and conscientiously, his stature as the ultimate states-man of the blues growing as the years went by. In the 1970s Waters began working with guitarist and producer Johnny Winter, and his album "Hard Again" gave us the blues classic "Mannish Boy." In 1978 he sang this song in the live concert film *The Last Waltz*, delivering what was perhaps the best performance of the evening. Waters also continued touring, both at home and abroad, at times doing a phenomenal three hundred shows a year.

And it was evident that Waters savored his success. When asked if he looked back with nostalgia at his early days in Mississippi and Chicago, Waters answered with an emphatic "no." He went on to say:

> I'm out there workin' as much as I want to, turnin' down jobs I could be doin', and the money's up. These records I'm making now, that Johnny Winter's producing, they're sellin' better than any of my old records ever did. . . . I'll tell you the truth: this is the best point of my life that I'm livin' now.

And did he regret that he'd had to work so long and so hard to achieve his success?

"Feels good," Waters answered. "Are you kiddin'? I'm glad it came before I died, I can tell you. Feels great."[6]

Waters's own work remains staggering and impressive. He remains one of the supreme blues masters. So long was his shadow, so powerful was the formula he invented, that he spawned innumerable imitators. The sheer force of his music seemed to suggest to these musicians that Muddy's way was the only way to play the blues.

Nothing, of course, could have been further from the truth. Previous to Waters there had been, as we've seen, a vast variety of blues types: some blues preached plainly religious themes and some spoke of hard times, some were played solo and some were played by bands, some were played in unusual time signatures, some quietly and some as loud as a locomotive. Yet Waters's influence was so great that after him, a sad and predictable uniformity sometimes settled upon the blues. Rather than charting new ground, established and new musicians seemed satisfied simply to imitate Waters, and if not Waters, then the next great guitarist in line, B. B. King. Soon, almost every blues song sung or recorded bore Waters's distinctive stamp. Much of this uniformity has lasted, more or less, to this day. Most blues bands and musicians continue to play electric instruments in 4/4 time at high volume, their AAB pattern lyrics rarely departing from the themes of sexual boasting or betrayal that Waters favored. As a result, the blues have sometimes been accused by those who are familiar only with Waters and his imitators as being predictable, uninspired, even boring. A good listen to Leadbelly, Robert Johnson, or Bessie Smith would instantly dispel this impression.

Of course, it wasn't Waters's fault that he'd created a style of music so infectious that few musicians could resist it. Waters's genuis was that he developed a musical style clearly and particularly his own: his imitators were responsible for transforming his personal innovations into the formula that recent blues have sometimes become.

Muddy Waters died in Chicago on April 30, 1983. His funeral was attended by more than a thousand mourners.

The Sixties
"Revival"

At their first American press conference, the Beatles were asked what they most wanted to see now that they were in the country that had given birth to rock 'n' roll.

"Muddy Waters and Bo Diddley," they answered.

"Where's that?" asked a thoroughly unenlightened reporter.

The Beatles rolled their eyes. "You Americans don't seem to know your most famous citizens," John Lennon said.[1]

This was in 1963. By this time, the blues were beginning to be heard the world over, although obviously not everyone in the United States had paid attention to this phenomenon. If there was any question concerning the rising popularity and cultural significance of the blues, though, it was surely put to rest at this press conference.

The Beatles were referring to American musicians who would later be called part of the "blues revival" of the 1960s. It was at this time that the blues, already having been around for some sixty years, were "discovered" and appreciated by a wider, whiter, and more affluent audience. This was primarily the result of an explosion of blues interest in England. Thanks to a vanguard of London-based musicians, including the Rolling Stones and Eric Clapton, this new popularity eventually made its way back across the Atlantic where a number of older African-American blues musicians gained the recognition, if not always the financial reward, they had long deserved. Soon, blues players could be found across the country, performing in Greenwich Village coffee shops, university auditoriums, and local music festivals.

This movement is clearly an important chapter in the history of the blues; never before had so many people been exposed to its sound and message. But using the term "revival" to describe this period is misleading. It suggests that the blues had somehow "died out" sometime after its early days, only to be "rediscovered" in the early 1960s by white musicians, intellectuals, and music critics. This scenario is simply not true. As the careers of Leadbelly, Billie Holiday, and Muddy Waters have shown, the blues continued to be performed by musicians of vast talent and listened to by many. Meanwhile, many lesser-known but equally talented musicians also kept working throughout the United States. Performers as diverse as Chester "Howlin' Wolf" Burnett, "Blind" Reverend Gary Davis, "Sleepy" John Estes, "Mississippi" John Hurt, Jimmy Rushing, and even the older blues master Eddie "Son" House, all maintained, and even improved, their craft during this supposedly fallow time.

The blues, in short, had never gone away. They were not necessarily found in every record store, or played on every radio station, or whistled on teenagers' lips. Yet they were always there, being pounded out in nightclubs, apartments, and shotgun shacks.

It was just that it took awhile for the rest of the world to figure out how to have that much fun.

The city of London, and its miles of surrounding suburbs, is literally and metaphorically on the other side of the world from the rural American South, the birthplace of the blues. Driving through the endless neighborhoods of tidy houses with perfectly manicured gardens, and then through the sooty, working-class boroughs that make up this sprawling metropolis, you won't find a single cotton field, sharecropper's shack, or lazy, dusty road disappearing into the sweltering sunset. And in one especially important way, London in the early 1960s did not even resemble Memphis or Chicago, those other cities that had played such an important part in the development of the blues. Simply put, there were few black people in London. There were even fewer African-Americans, and at the time—without exaggeration—not a single, professional African-American blues musician called London home.

So how was it that this seemingly unlikely place was to become the starting point for a musical revolution, a revolution that would eventually help make the blues heard around the world?

First of all, we can't forget that the blues are an art form. In this way, just like any other art form, they are not necessarily limited to a single place, a single time, or even a single race. Although the blues rose out of specific geographic, social, and economic conditions, the blues form is at once so powerful and accessible that it can be learned and played by almost anyone, at any time. Of course, this accessibility does not guarantee the quality of the resulting product. It's unlikely that a musician who is unfamiliar with the background of the blues could still play them with the passion of Robert Johnson or Muddy Waters. Nevertheless, the blues in certain ways do exist, and can even thrive, far beyond the time and place of its roots. As Robert Cray, one of today's most esteemed bluesmen puts it, "Anybody can sing the blues. . . . I wasn't born in the South and I didn't pick cotton. I like to sing this music because it's about real-life situations."[2]

The promise of freedom, as always, was another one of the attractions of the blues. Obviously, "freedom" for young white men and women in postwar Britain meant something much different than it meant for blacks in the American South. There were no prison chain gangs in England, no segregated classrooms, no murderous hate groups. Yet England did have its own brand of oppression. British society was at the time strictly divided upon class lines. In other words, the rich stayed with the rich, and the poor stayed with the poor. The clothes you wore, the way you spoke, where you came from—all of these were an indication of your status in society, and you were supposed to behave in the way thought fitting to your class. Everyone in England was thought to have been born into a certain place in society, and having been born into this place you were not supposed to rise above it.

Not surprisingly, there was a great deal of resentment toward this rigid social code. And the blues were a well-suited avenue for the expression of this anger and frustration. Surely, if a black blues singer in the United States had the courage to sing about his or her merciless treatment at the hands of whites, couldn't a young Englishperson vent his or her fury as well? If Bessie Smith could point an accusing finger at the rich, weren't there equally spoiled targets asking for it in England, hidden behind the ivy-covered walls of their country estates? When looked at in this way, it almost seems strange that the blues did not catch on sooner in England.

This doesn't mean that there aren't some problems with the thought of middle-class English white boys—or middle-class American white boys, for that matter—picking up on, imitating, and then making money off the work of lesser-known, less financially privileged blacks. The young London lads discussed in this chapter, whatever indignities they might have suffered, never faced the kind of deprivation and degradation that haunted Huddie Ledbetter and Blind Lemon Jefferson. Yet the enraptured, eager Londoners we are going to meet never claimed to have invented the blues: to their credit, they always cited their sources, always were ready to point out they were simply following in some already prodigious footsteps. In their youthful enthusiasm they virtually worshiped the African-American blues musicians who had preceded them. Howlin' Wolf, Chuck Berry, Bo Diddley, Muddy Waters, Big Bill Broonzey: these names gave off an honored, magical ring, and no young British musician of the time ever hoped to surpass them. Learn from them, emulate them, yes—but surpass them, never.

The Rolling Stones

It has become the stuff of legend.

One morning in 1960, Mike Jagger, age eighteen, was riding a train across London. Rows of tenements flew past outside the windows. At each station, quiet, shuffling crowds of polite Londoners boarded the train, got off at the next stop, and from there trudged to work under the gray skies. Looking out the window, Mike Jagger (he had yet to start calling himself Mick) fit right in with this workaday crowd. At the time he was a promising young student at the London School of Economics: pale, good at mathematics, the son of a physical education instructor, dressed in the standard uniform of the time—a dark jacket and tie. Nothing would single him out from other commuters that morning.

Except for one thing. Under his arm, he held his brand-new copy of Chuck Berry's latest record, *Rocking at the Hop*.

Strictly speaking, Chuck Berry was not a blues artist. Rock 'n' roll was Berry's medium, but for the young Jagger, Berry had all the necessary credentials: he was from America, he was black, and his music was raw, passionate, and thrilling. Just recently, Jagger had been turned on to this brand of American music by a friend, Dick Taylor. Together they had listened to all the American rock and blues records they could find. At the time this was no small trick, considering that such music could only be found on import albums: no British recording company thought it worthwhile to sign up blues artists. So together Jagger and Taylor crisscrossed London, rooting through record shops, bringing home all of this music they could find. It was the blues singers—Jimmy Reed and Chester "Howlin' Wolf" Burnett, in particular—who impressed Jagger the most. So much so that in their spare time he and Dick got together and played with a few friends who called themselves "Little Boy Blue and the Blue Boys." They devoted themselves, as their name so doggedly suggested, solely to the blues. They were, by all accounts, a terribly awkward little band, and their sole audience was Dick Taylor's mother, who had the patience to let the boys practice in her living room.

Jagger went on looking out the window.

The train stopped at Dartford Station.

That's where another young man, pimply, pitifully thin, and jug eared, got on. His name was Keith Richard.

Richard recognized Jagger immediately. Years before they had gone to the same grammar school, but since then Richard's life had followed a path much different than Jagger's. Jagger's family was middle class; Richard's family was working class. Richard lived in a government-funded housing project; his father worked in a lightbulb factory, his mother in a bakery. Richard's neighborhood was tough, and one of the few solaces in his life was playing the guitar. This seemed, to all those around him, to be a waste of time since they thought he couldn't get steady work just playing the guitar. Unlike Jagger, there seemed to be nothing so prestigious as the London School of Economics in his future. Richard had, in fact, just been expelled from Dartford Technical School for truancy.

A little intimidated by the sight of Jagger in his proper tie and jacket, it's likely that Richard would have given him little more than a passing nod, except for the fact that Jagger was carrying a Chuck Berry album. Richard idolized Chuck Berry, and, summoning up his courage, he pointed at the record and spoke to Jagger.

"Ey, there. Wotcha got?"

Jagger showed Richard his record, and, realizing they shared the same taste in music, they struck up a conversation, which in turn led to a friendship, which in turn would lead to their forming what some have called the greatest band in the history of rock 'n' roll.

The fact that Jagger and Richard were to become the main creative forces behind the Rolling Stones is, of course, well known. What is less well known, though, is that they initially saw themselves, first and last, as a blues band. It was the music they loved, and along with the other members of the band—Brian Jones, Bill Wyman, and Charlie Watts—they were committed to playing this extraordinary brand of African-American music. The name "The Rolling Stones" came, in fact,

The Rolling Stones perform on a British TV show in June 1963. The Stones, who took their name from the lyrics of a Muddy Waters song, helped popularize the blues and introduced white audiences to the music of Waters, Howlin' Wolf, and other blues greats.

from a Muddy Waters song, the only problem with it being that Jagger was afraid it might give the wrong impression to those who weren't up on blues trivia. "I hope they don't think we're a rock and roll outfit," Jagger said before one of their early gigs.[3]

Jagger and Richard, though, weren't the only English musicians at this time to be in love with this music. Although still in the minority, others had fallen under the spell of the blues—to the point that a genuine movement was getting under way. In the late 1950s, a London guitarist named Alexis Korner had put together an all-acoustic group called Blues Incorporated, for which Mick Jagger had been an early singer. Meanwhile, across town, Mick Fleetwood had formed a band called Fleetwood Mac. Long before they were to become a sensation in the 1970s, this band was playing the blues in the few London bars that would have them. Eric Burden, John Mayall, Jeff Beck, Steve Winwood, Jimmy Page—all of these English musicians, who would later play such an important part in transforming rock 'n' roll, were early blues enthusiasts. Also among this group was a pasty-faced boy named Eric Clapton, who would later emerge as one of the greatest blues guitarists of all time. But more about Clapton in a little while.

The Stones, busy themselves, had secured a regular Sunday night slot at a small venue called the Crawdaddy Club. To the surprise of everyone involved—especially considering that many in their audience had probably never heard of the blues—they were an unqualified hit. Inspired by the American musicians they so admired, the Stones's music was powerful, genuine, reckless, a little dangerous. This seemed to be exactly what the London teenagers who crowded into that cramped, dark, damp club wanted to hear. The audience was no doubt responding to the same liberating aspect of the blues that had been so initially attractive to Jagger and Richard: here was music you could dance to, make love to, shout about. Instead of sugarcoated pop songs, which were so much the rage at the time, the Stones were playing music that was fierce, openhearted, and desperate. Many who came to these early gigs, maybe even the Stones themselves, didn't completely understand exactly how fierce, openhearted, and desperate these songs really were. Did these London adolescents know that Leadbelly's "Midnight Special" was actually a lament on suicide? Did they know that Lonnie Johnson's "Careless Love" was really about the ravages of syphilis and murder?[4] Probably not. Still, they were responding to the unvarnished, truth-telling *spirit* of the blues, which rose up through the music, regardless if they were completely aware of all the specifics. This was the real thing, and everybody knew it.

As the Stones's popularity grew—through record contracts, tours of Europe and the United States, and appearances on such influential television programs as the *Ed Sullivan Show*—gradually their music had less and less to do with the blues. A number of the songs soon to be written by Jagger and Richard—such as "As Tears Go By," "Ruby Tuesday," and "Play With Fire"—had little in common with the blues. Nevertheless, countless other songs—"Honky Tonk Woman," "Satisfaction," "Gimme Shelter," "Sympathy for the Devil," and "Rip This Joint," for example—reflect both a lasting musical and philosophical connection to the blues. These songs are unabashed treatments of sexuality, social cruelty, and the simple power of music itself—themes that are all common to the blues. The Rolling Stones were able to blend their blues and rock influences into a powerful musical amalgam uniquely their own, which is often imitated today.

Strictly as blues musicians, the Stones's greatest accomplishment was probably that they, more than anyone else, were the ones who made the blues popular. For example, when they appeared on the then widely watched British television music program *Ready, Steady, Go* on November 20, 1964, they performed a little-known blues song called "Little Red Rooster." Written by Willie Dixon, and first performed by Chester "Howlin' Wolf" Burnett, "Little Red Rooster" was a flat-out bold blues number. As thousands of viewers across the country sat around their black-and-white television sets, watching these long-haired boys play this amazing music, a new age in the history of the blues had begun. "Little Red Rooster" shot to the top of the charts in England, and the blues became a household word.

This brilliant music was no longer only known by African-Americans and a handful of white enthusiasts. Thanks in large part to the Stones, who, as mentioned, always gave credit where credit was due, the blues became a financial and popular juggernaut, reaching audiences the world over. A tremendous ripple effect was created by this upsurge in blues popularity: black musicians began appearing more widely in Europe, while back in the United States many blues performers who had struggled in relative obscurity now found that they could play almost wherever and whenever they wished. Not since the 1920s, when record company scouts roamed the American South looking for the next Blind Lemon Jefferson and Bessie Smith, had the blues been so popular. The irony, of course, is that the Stones succeeded in making the blues popular not only because they were immensely talented but also because they were white. Being white, they were, sadly, more "acceptable" to white audiences of the time, who then in turn sought out the original music and musicians upon which the Stones had based so much of their work. Many African-American musicians were equally as talented as the Rolling Stones: in fact, Chester Burnett's vocal rendition of "Little Red Rooster" makes Jagger's attempt sound positively frail. Nevertheless, given the ingrained racism of the early 1960s, it is unlikely that it could have happened any other way. This blues "revival" was indeed due in large part to the brilliant work of white musicians. Yet it should be remembered that without the pioneering labor of hundreds of earlier black artists, there would have been nothing to "revive" in the first place.

Eric Clapton

There's a hilarious photograph of Eric Clapton taken in the spring of 1963, not long after Jagger and Richard ran into each other on that fateful day. The picture shows Clapton on stage with his first band, the Roosters. No one in the group looks much like a "blues musician." They're white teenagers. The singer, though, at least looks a little tough. Holding the microphone with an obviously practiced casualness, he seems to be trying to project the street savvy usually associated with the blues. The drummer, his back against the wall, adds something to the band simply because he's handsome. With the bass player, though, we start to get on shaky ground: he looks like he probably had to skip school to make this gig, and he's wearing a pair of uncool horn-rimmed glasses—but then so did Buddy Holly.

Finally, on the other side of the drummer, stands Clapton, picking his guitar. With his narrow tie, plaid jacket, and polished wing-tipped shoes, he has all the swagger of a nervous chemistry student. Worst of all is the expression on his face: he's got a big, goofy grin that seems to shout, "Gee, it's fun to play with you guys!" Everything about him says that he belongs at home, having tea with mom and dad, not out late at night in some blues band. Where's that rugged blues attitude? You won't find it on Clapton, not yet anyway. For the time being, in this photograph, he can't pretend to be anyone other than himself. There he is, Eric Clapton, 1963: a skinny English boy, in love with the blues.

Oddly enough, these apparently awkward qualities would eventually lead Clapton to the heights of fame. Unlike the other members of the Roosters, Clapton, even at this early stage in his career, seems both burdened and blessed, above all, with honesty. Even in this early photograph, he seems unable to strike a pose, to act a part, to be anyone other than himself. He's excited by the music, and his face shows it— regardless of whether this looks "cool" or not. In this photograph, we can already see in Clapton his embrace of the music he most cares about, even if it is music that is less than popular, even if it is music that can't guarantee you'll get rich playing it, even if, in the eyes of some, you'll wind up looking like a grinning fool.

Eric Clapton was born on March 30, 1945, in Ripley, England.[5] Later in life, Clapton would come to greatly admire Robert Johnson, who, like Clapton, was an illegitimate child.

When Eric was born, his mother, Pat, was sixteen and unmarried. His father, meanwhile, a soldier by the name of Edward Fryer, didn't want anything to do with his young child and so left England for Canada. Uncertain as to whether she could properly care for Eric, Pat asked her mother, Rose, if Eric could live with her. Rose Clapton agreed. Eric was given her last name, and he grew up in her house, under her care.

Like so many other musicians, Eric was fascinated by music early on. He knew he wanted to be a musician by the age of six, when he started playing the recorder, a kind of simplified clarinet, in his school band. As he got older he started listening to all the rock and blues records he could get his hands on. He persuaded his grandmother to buy him a guitar, and as he sat on the top steps of her house—he liked to play there because the stairwell gave his music what he felt was a nice echo—he taught himself all the guitar parts from his records. This single-minded commitment did have consequences, though. Eric was spending so much time playing music that he neglected his schoolwork and was expelled at seventeen.

Being expelled had its drawbacks, but it at least gave Eric more time to work on his guitar playing. Soon he had joined up with four other blues lovers. They put a band together and called themselves "The Roosters," presumably after the song "Little Red Rooster," which, as we've already seen, was a tune that impressed the Rolling Stones. Like most beginning efforts, the Roosters weren't particularly successful. They dearly loved playing the blues—which was starting to become a genuine phenomenon among young London rockers—but they weren't particularly skilled. After playing only a handful of gigs, mostly at private parties, the group broke up. Clapton, though, emerged as the best musician in the band, and he was soon working with another group—the one that would make him famous.

Unlike the Roosters, the Yardbirds were professionals. They soon attracted a devoted following as they played their version of British blues in a number of London clubs. In fact, when the Stones had finished up their now infamous stint at the

Crawdaddy Club, they were replaced by the Yardbirds, who soon were bringing in even bigger crowds than the Stones had. Likewise, they secured a record contract and began touring throughout England. As in every group of which he was a part, it was Clapton's now mature, passionate guitar playing that was the band's main attraction. It was quickly becoming obvious that for Clapton, the blues weren't just a passing fad, weren't just an attitude to try on: he was playing with all his heart and all his soul. The blues spoke to him, seemed to explain his life to him, and he wanted to communicate this deep satisfaction that he'd found. Perhaps it was the fact that he had only occasionally seen his mother while he'd been growing up; perhaps it was the fact that his father had more or less deserted him from the day of his birth—but for whatever reason, Clapton not only played the blues, he seemed to have them, too. Once again, his honesty was showing.

But the very aspects of Clapton's personality that helped make him a virtuoso musician weren't helping him get along with the other members of his band. For the most part, the other Yardbirds were all thrilled about their dizzying success. They had already put out two hit singles, had performed with the Beatles at that group's annual Christmas concert, and seemed poised on the brink of genuine stardom. But Clapton wasn't satisfied. A perfectionist, he would frequently criticize the other members of the band, especially when he believed they weren't playing as well as they should. He was moody, didn't particularly like the new material the band was trying out, and he told everyone about it. Clapton thought the band was becoming too commercial and was starting to give up on the blues in favor of a more pop sound.

It was at this time, in February 1964, that Clapton's own dream of a lifetime was fulfilled. Muddy Waters was in London to record an album, and to Clapton's delight, he was invited to play on two tracks: "Pretty Girls Everywhere" and "Stir Me Up." To sit across from this blues giant was, for Clapton, like being in guitar heaven. Here, at last, were the real blues, being played by one of its masters. This was no imitation. It didn't make him much money; there were no

The Yardbirds, featuring Eric Clapton
(1945–   ), right, on guitar

screaming fans—but the music was honest. When Clapton returned to the band, inspired by his sessions with Waters, he was all the more committed to staying true to his blues roots. The rest of the Yardbirds, though, had other ideas.

Bassist Paul Samwell-Smith had brought in a new song called "For Your Love," suggesting that it be the group's next single. Although catchy, Clapton thought that the song was childish pop, one that could have been performed by a dozen other bands. Reluctantly, he went along and performed the song, but he was disgusted with the final recording. Featuring the dulcet tones of a harpsichord, an instrument that was, inexplicably, all the rage at the time, "For Your Love" simply didn't have any of the hard-driving blues feel that had made the Yardbirds popular in the first place. Nevertheless, the song instantly shot to number one on the British charts, and it continues to be played on radio stations to this day. The song's popularity didn't matter to Clapton, though. He felt the song was a sellout. He left the band, and music magazines and newspapers shouted the headline: "Clapton Quits Yardbirds— Too Commercial!"

By now, famous for his guitar technique, Clapton didn't have to look far for another group eager to have him on lead. He soon joined up with John Mayall, who shared Clapton's commitment to the blues, and became the guitar player in Mayall's band, the Bluesbreakers. Twelve years older than Clapton, Mayall had been playing the blues, mostly on the keyboards, all his professional life. In Mayall, Clapton had found what he thought was a real musical partner.

It was during his time with Mayall's band that Clapton sealed his reputation as one of the greatest blues guitarists of all time. Although few had thought it possible, his playing surpassed the work he'd done with the Yardbirds; and as a result, Clapton gained a huge cult following. All over London, you could see the words "Clapton Is God" spray-painted on subway station walls, in the restrooms at the clubs where the Bluesbreakers played, and across the backs of the leather jackets worn by Clapton's die-hard fans. More than likely, it was the sheer emotion with which Clapton played that made his playing so attractive and extraordinary. Unlike Muddy

Waters—or Jimi Hendrix, for that matter, who would later in the decade prove himself to be a brilliant blues player as well—Clapton was not, in a technical sense, an innovator. He was not in the forefront of playing amplified blues; he did not introduce any particular time signature or standardize any band format; he did not employ the relatively unexplored effects of guitar feedback, as Hendrix did. Instead, Clapton's technical mastery, and in this way he is similar to Louis Armstrong, was always used to bring out the particular blues *feeling* of a song: that sense of agony, loss, and ultimately, hard-won triumph.

Clapton's ability to convey feeling came from his essential honesty, from expecting the best from himself and being satisfied with nothing less. Unlike so many other rock stars, Clapton frequently shunned the spotlight, always trying to concentrate on the quality of his music rather than on its commercial appeal. When he was playing the blues, Clapton seemed to be on a personal quest—one in which his own worth as a musician, and perhaps even as a person, depended on how well he played his last solo. With the stakes so high, no wonder his London fans revered him.

Despite the level of quality their music had reached, rifts were developing among the Bluesbreakers. As he had done with the Yardbirds, Clapton criticized the Bluesbreakers for falling back upon its now tried-and-true numbers, rather than trying out new songs and staking out new ground. The fact was, the band's other musicians weren't as skilled as Clapton—and while they were doing all they could to keep up with him, Clapton was getting bored. In July 1966, with a hit album on the charts, and the Bluesbreakers at the top of their commercial success, Clapton quit the band.

Clapton put together his next band, Cream, with the thought of becoming more experimental with his music. Perhaps understandably, given his ambition and interests, Clapton now chose to play music far outside the strict, purist blues tradition he had up to then so championed. And although Cream, with drummer Ginger Baker and bassist Jack Bruce, was a critical and commercial success, Clapton's work in the band marks the end of his career as a pure blues player.

With Cream, Clapton would explore the then-popular "psychedelic" sound. Later, in the 1970s as a solo performer, he would also find inspiration in such wide-ranging styles as country-western and reggae, evidenced by his now famous renditions of "Tulsa Time" and Bob Marley's "I Shot the Sheriff." Nevertheless, throughout his career, Clapton has often returned to his roots in the blues. In his appearance on *MTV Unplugged*, the recording of which would become his best-selling album, Clapton performed a number of songs written by his idol Robert Johnson, and Clapton's 1994 album *From the Cradle* is all blues; it features some of the fiercest blues guitar playing to be found anywhere.

The stories concerning Clapton's personal life are often discussed more than his music. As with other performers, such as Billie Holiday and Leadbelly, these stories can sometimes overshadow the musician's achievements. Like Holiday and Leadbelly, Eric Clapton has led an often turbulent life. In the late 1960s he developed a near-deadly heroin addiction; at the same time he experienced the loss of his good friends Jimi Hendrix and Duane Allman (Hendrix apparently died from complications from a drug overdose, and Allman perished in a motorcycle accident); and his marriages were often fraught with difficulty. In 1991 his young son, Conor, died from an accidental fall from an apartment window. Clearly, Clapton, despite his success as a musician, has not had an easy life, and it would be easy to claim that this personal pain has made Clapton such an outstanding blues artist. This explanation is too simple, though. No doubt, as with all great musicians, Clapton's artistry comes not only from life experiences and talent but also from unceasing commitment to work at his music. You can't be a great player without work, and who knows how much more work Clapton could have done had not drugs and other unfortunate events in his life gotten in his way.

Thanks to bands such as the Rolling Stones and individual musicians such as Clapton, the blues had reached an unprecedented level of popularity by the mid-1960s. The wave that had started in England soon reached the United

States, where the blues had begun. As I've said, this change in fortune was a help for many African-American blues musicians. Thanks to the increased commercial appeal of the blues, a number of musical careers were either resurrected or given the boost of a lifetime. Sadly, these original blues players never received the level of financial success or popular attention that had come the way of their white prodigies. Nevertheless, the music, as always, was the most important thing, and, commercial concerns aside, these African-American players continued to practice and improve their craft.

Sam "Lightnin'" Hopkins and John Lee Hooker

Two of the most important American blues players to achieve national and international recognition thanks to this new interest in the blues were Sam "Lightnin'" Hopkins and John Lee Hooker.

There is an unusual degree of similarity between the careers of these men: both found new prominence in the early 1960s and both were equally adept at playing both acoustic and electric guitars, either in solo work or in fronting their own bands. In these ways they represent the last present link we have to the original style of deep Southern blues as created by Patton, House, and Johnson. After Hopkins and Hooker, the majority of blues musicians have continued to follow in Waters's footsteps, working almost exclusively in electric, band-based styles. Although it is certainly possible that some younger musician will resurrect this older—and, in my estimation, often the more expressive—tradition, for the moment Hopkins (who died in 1982) and Hooker (who only recently retired from active touring) remain unparalleled in their ability to master both the newer "urban" blues and the traditional "country" blues.

Lightnin' Hopkins, the older of the two, was born in Centerville, Texas, in 1912.[6] He learned to play guitar from his older brother, Joel, and in 1920, at the age of eight, he played alongside Blind Lemon Jefferson at a country picnic. As

113

legend has it, Jefferson was playing propped up on the end of a field wagon, which was being used as a makeshift stage. Between songs, he heard someone playing the guitar behind him. Jefferson, duly impressed with the music he heard and obviously unable to see that this musician was just a boy, invited the young Hopkins to join him up on the wagon. It was not until they'd played a few songs together that Lemon, to his laughter and amazement, was told that he'd been performing with a child.

However precocious Hopkins's ability might have been—and it's a little hard to believe that a professional such as Jefferson would have been so completely fooled by an eight-year-old—he was clearly a gifted musician. As he grew older, a hallmark of his playing was his deceptively casual, offhand rambling style. Hopkins had so many riffs, chord progressions, lyrical themes, and rhythms committed to memory that he could spontaneously string together any number of these elements, inventing a song on the spot, adding or subtracting verses and improvising rhymes as he saw fit. This was another direct link Hopkins had to the older blues musicians, who would often play together for their own entertainment, trading songs and stories and whiskey as the day wore on.

At some point in the mid-1930s, Hopkins was sent to a prison work farm—the crime he committed is not known, although the short time he spent in prison suggests that it was probably a minor offense—and after his release he began touring across east Texas. This work eventually landed him a recording contract, and throughout the 1940s and 1950s, Hopkins cut sides with a variety of record companies. With these recordings, he was well on his way to being acknowledged as the most frequently recorded blues musician of all time.

The late 1950s, though, were difficult for Hopkins. It was at this time that the Chicago blues sound was beginning to reign supreme, and though Hopkins was well acquainted with electric styles (his song "Play With Your Poodle" is, in fact, an early piece of amplified rock 'n' roll), his records had never sold particularly well. Respectable sales, sure, but nothing outstanding, and as a result record companies became

Sam "Lightnin'" Hopkins (1912–82),
one of the greatest blues improvisators

increasingly hesitant to hire this once-prolific artist. Without income from record sales, Hopkins moved to Houston, Texas, where he played at house parties and rented a small apartment. It seemed as if the Chicago train, with all its thunder and glory, was going to pass him by.

It was there, in Houston, that an emissary of the blues revival tracked him down. This was the scholar and historian Sam Charters, who, along with Alan Lomax, remains one of the most influential writers to document the blues and bring them to greater public attention. After following lead after lead, hunting for Hopkins all over Houston, Charters at last found him in his tiny apartment. Charters had brought along a reel-to-reel tape recorder, and after a little discussion, Hopkins agreed to play for Charters. In the course of a few hours, with a bottle of gin on the floor between them, and with Charters alternatively holding the microphone to Hopkins's mouth when he sang and to the guitar when he played, Sam Hopkins created one of the genuine masterpieces of the blues.

The sound of the album *Lightnin' Hopkins* is simple. It is Hopkins alone, talking, singing, and playing his guitar, and yet the songs express a wide and desperate range of emotions, all delivered in a sparse, direct, and sometimes chilling manner. From "Penetentiary Blues" to "Trouble Stay Away from My Door" to "Come Go Home with Me"—in song after song Hopkins presents an unvarnished allegory of his life, one of suffering, resignation, and survival, which finally builds to the album's climax, a scant two-minute, five-second version of the old Blind Lemon Jefferson song "See That My Grave Is Kept Clean."

> *There's two white horses in a line,*
> *Two white horses in a line,*
> *Two white horses, two white horses,*
> *Takin' me to the burying ground*

Singing from the point of view of a corpse, Hopkins's voice is husky, ashen, and pure, as if he is truly speaking from beyond the grave. Few recorded blues performances equal this one in its directness, simplicity, and heartbreak.

When he'd run out of tape, Charters knew that Hopkins had just laid down a tremendous work. He immediately set out to get Hopkins a new recording contract, based upon the obvious strength of this spontaneous session. Unlike Hopkins, Charters was aware that there was a growing interest in this style of unadorned folk blues, and soon Charters arranged for this taped afternoon to be released as an album. It was received to great acclaim and proved to be a turning point in Hopkins's life. From then until the end of his life, Hopkins remained an essential figure on the blues scene, one of its authentic masters.

John Lee Hooker, eight years younger than Hopkins, was to have a steadier, and, later in life, a more financially lucrative career.[7] Neverthless, the parallels between Hooker and Hopkins persist. If Hopkins's connection to the early blues came by way of his encounter with Blind Lemon Jefferson, Hooker's connection was given to him at the moment of his birth. Hooker was born in Clarksdale, Mississippi, a town in the middle of that fertile patch of ground just south of Memphis that has produced, per square acre, more prodigious musicians than any other similarly sized area in the country. Like Hopkins, Hooker is adept at playing in a number of styles, in a number of musical configurations, sometimes solo and sometimes with his own band.

Hooker's style, however, is less improvisatory, less spontaneous than Hopkins's. Instead, Hooker often opts for a thumping, persistent, one-chord riff played over a sustained, pulsing rhythm, sometimes beat out by a drummer and sometimes by Hooker's own stamping foot. His distinctive voice is deep, weathered, and rough, sometimes reaching notes so low as to become no more than an ominous, poisonous croak. This combination of Hooker's distinctively rhythmic playing and his dark, forbidding voice made him immediately stand out from other blues players and was used to great effect on his classic 1949 recording "Boogie Chillun." To Hooker's surprise, this song reached number one on the rhythm-and-blues charts and is today considered a blues standard.

Hooker moved to Detroit, Michigan, in 1943, lured out of the South like so many other African-Americans by the promise of employment. It was there that Hooker began to establish himself. Again like Hopkins, he made a name for himself primarily through voluminous recording sessions. Just as they do today, most record companies required artists to sign "exclusive" contracts, meaning that the artist could record only for that company. Hooker, bursting with more musical ideas and energy than any single company could handle, found a means of circumventing these exclusive contracts by signing with other companies under assumed names. In the 1940s and 1950s, Hooker recorded under the names Birmingham Sam, Delta Bob, Texas Slim, Johnny Lee, Johnny Williams, Boogie Man, and John Lee Booker. Hooker didn't seem to care about drawing attention to these ploys and any possible legal ramifications they might entail: regardless of the name he used, his music was invariably and obviously his own, the same John Lee Hooker pounding out his riffs and growling his lyrics. Anyone with any knowledge of the Detroit, or even Midwest, blues scene would have instantly recognized each of these imaginery players as being Hooker.

Unlike Hopkins, Hooker's career never went through a serious slump. He continued to work and record steadily, his reputation increased by the commercial success of "Boogie Chillun'." Nevertheless, the new blues interest of the 1960s secured Hooker a place in the public imagination. He toured Europe in 1962 and performed at the historic Newport Folk Festival in 1960 and 1963 and at the Newport Jazz Festival in 1964. He returned to play Europe every year between 1964 and 1969; meanwhile, his popularity increased in the States. For many who saw him play, Hooker, alone on a stage, hunched over his guitar, seemed to be the ideal haunting and powerful blues figure.

And still Hooker's star continued to rise. In the 1970s he recorded with the blues rock band Canned Heat while continuing to tour on his own. He made a brief appearance in

John Lee Hooker (1920–) is shown in 1994. Hooker's foot-stomping song "Boogie Chillun" climbed to number one on the rhythm-and-blues charts in 1949; forty years later his star-studded album, The Healer, *won a Grammy Award as the best blues album of 1989.*

the film *The Blues Brothers*, and then, in 1989 he released one of the most popular blues albums of all time, *The Healer*. Playing with Hooker on the album were such admiring and diverse musicians as Bonnie Raitt, Carlos Santana, George Thoroughgood, and Robert Cray. *The Healer*, which won the Grammy that year for the best blues album, introduced a whole new generation to the power of the blues.

Hooker retired from touring in 1993 but continues to record. He now lives in Los Angeles. Along with B. B. King, he is one of the reigning elder statesmen of the blues.

With the life of John Lee Hooker, we're now up to the blues of today. Still, there's a part of the story of the blues that we haven't yet touched on. Precisely what is it about the blues that have drawn so many people to them as a musical form? What is it about this music that inspires so much interest and admiration, causing musicians to devote their lives to playing it and causing blues historians to haggle over such seemingly arcane matters as determining the exact circumstances leading up to Huddie Ledbetter's first run-in with the law?

In other words, what is so special about the blues?

In the next chapter I'll try to explain at least some of the attraction by examining the meaning implicit in the blues: meaning that is rarely expressed but that nevertheless runs through the music like a backbone.

Meaning in the Blues

The blues is an impulse to keep the painful details of a brutal experience alive in one's aching consciousness, to finger its jagged grain, and to transcend it, not by the consolation of philosophy but by squeezing from it a near-tragic, near-comic lyricism.[1]

—Ralph Ellison

At the beginning of this book, I made the claim that the blues are more than just music—that they also present a way of looking at the world. To me, the blues clearly represent an avenue of both literal and psychological liberation for African-Americans. Without question, the blues did and do provide an enormous meaning to black Americans, as well as to anyone who listens.

But the blues outlook is more complex than this. It is not, of course, a rigid, rule-bound philosophy. No one, no blues musician or scholar, has consciously sat down and decided that the blues mean *this* and don't mean *that*, that the blues should be listened to for one reason rather than another. The blues outlook is shifting and improvised, without a single author, created by a combination of circumstance and talent,

121

modified and redefined as the need arises. There are, nevertheless, certain central ideas that run throughout the blues and that account for much of the blues's enormous appeal.

First of all, let's take the word the "blues" itself. By definition, this word means sadness, loss, and pain. But what could possibly be so attractive about sadness, loss, and pain? Why sit around, as many people obviously do, and listen to music where someone is wailing about the difficulty of his or her fate? Aren't we looking for escape, happiness, and pleasure in the music we listen to?

Not necessarily.

The United States is, for the most part, a culture obsessed with comedy. We need to look no further for confirmation of this than to our television sets, where the most popular programs are invariably situation comedies. The supposedly more "serious" cops-and-robbers shows can be no more than live-action cartoons, where good always triumphs over evil, and where in the end everyone is usually left laughing about what a wild time they've all had while chasing down the crooks. And even when television movies take on more somber subjects, such as homelessness or a sensational case of kidnapping, these movies are almost invariably given "happy endings," where, even if the characters have had to struggle, we all know that in the end it will somehow turn out for the best. It is as if, through our popular culture, we are saying nothing bad ever happens in America. No one ever dies. No one ever suffers. And if you do suffer, take comfort in the knowledge that by the end of the half hour, someone is going to say something that will make you laugh so hard that you'll forget why you were crying.

Sooner or later, we're promised, Urkel will hitch up his pants, poke his horn-rimmed glasses, and act like an idiot.

In our hearts, though, we all know that life is nothing like this. In real life bad things happen: innocent children get caught in the crossfire of a drive-by shooting, Wall Street fat cats get slapped on the wrist for stealing other people's savings, an illness like AIDS can cut people down in the prime of life. In some ways, it makes sense that we would favor comic, escapist, and unreal forms of art and entertainment, where everything turns out all right in the end, where none of these worries exist, where every problem is solved in time for the commercial break.

Yet, with time, this solution grows thin. After awhile our continuously comic art begins to seem two-dimensional and meaningless—an elaborate sham—because we know it is not really telling the truth. It's like a drug: it might make you feel good for a minute or two, but all too soon you wake up, still facing the problems you tried so hard to escape.

So what does all this have to do with the blues?

In his book *Shadow and Act*, Ralph Ellison suggests that the blues are the one American art form capable of expressing genuine tragedy.[2] This statement is well worth examination. The blues, following Ellison's suggestion, are a kind of antidote to the falsely upbeat, falsely cheery drone of popular culture. The blues, as Ellison rightly points out, acknowledge that sometimes life is difficult, that sometimes harmful things do happen to people. Just as in classic Greek tragedy, lives can be torn apart, forgotten, forfeited, or destroyed. Robert Johnson does not get to go home again. The strange fruit of Billie Holiday's tree does not return to a blossom: it remains a tragic and mutilated body. No one can assure Blind Lemon Jefferson that his grave will be kept clean.

This may seem to be a forbidding, off-putting message. After all, there is a part of all of us that never wants to acknowledge tragic aspects of life. Yet, ultimately, the blues are a satifying and meaningful art form because they *do* acknowledge tragedy, because they do not flinch at admitting sad truths. Blues singer respects your intelligence: he or she does not try to fool you into believing something that you know is a lie. If I've got the courage to sing it, the blues singer says, then you surely have the courage to look at it.

In the end, the most enduring and meaningful comfort of all is not escape but knowing the truth.

And the blues will tell you the truth.

Because of their great capacity for truth telling, the blues have long been a form used by artists to examine and critique the society in which they live. If the blues tell the truth, however

The Reverend Gary Davis (1896–1972) performs in 1961. The blues have endured as an art form because blues songs tell the truth about life.

unsettling this truth might be, then they are a particularly useful tool in deciphering the lies that society may offer up as justifications for its own injustices. Take Bessie Smith's "Poor Man's Blues," for example. In this song Smith points out that society often claims that the poor are dependent upon the wealthy—for jobs, social benefits, and education. Yet Smith then turns the tables, revealing that the rich are equally dependent upon the poor—to fill their low-paying factory jobs, to clean their houses, to chauffeur their cars—and that our society is in part based upon this vast inequality between rich and poor.

In times of social discontent, such a critique has struck a deep chord with many Americans, black and white alike. And today this truth-telling spirit of the blues lives on in a number of forms. Although the rap group Public Enemy's music is only partially based upon the blues, their message is often the same—as in the song "911 Is a Joke." In this song rapper Chuck D points out that 911 emergency vehicles are sometimes more likely to respond to a call from a suburban neighborhood than to a call from an inner-city, African-American neighborhood. Such a practice is, of course, blatant and life-threatening discrimination. It flies in the face of the claim that we live in a free and equal society. Bessie Smith, we know, could have made this same point, some forty years ago. Although today's music sounds different than it did in Smith's time—with its sampled riffs, computer-produced rhythms, and multitrack effects—its spirit follows the long blues tradition of truthtelling.

It would be wrong, though, to suggest that the blues are solely concerned with somber subject matter. This is, in fact, one of the most common misconceptions people have about the blues: that they are exclusively concerned with pain and complaint. How else can you account for Chester "Howlin' Wolf" Burnett's openly gleeful "300 Pounds Of Joy," Louis Armstrong's delicately charming trumpet solos, and Bessie Smith's comic turn "Gimme A Pigfoot (And A Bottle of Beer)"? This last song comes from the same woman who gave us such a withering account of class relations in "Poor Man's Blues." If the blues are so tragic, how do you explain these plainly celebratory examples?

The fact is the blues are not a strictly tragic medium. Instead, they are realistic. Just as life is not always joyful, it is also not always painful. In even the most difficult times there are moments of happiness, humor, and absurdity. Robert Johnson, for example—who is one of the most stark of all blues musicians—recorded such bits of fluff as "Hot Tamales (They're Red Hot)," where he describes a woman who is so tall that "her head's in the bedroom and her feet's in the hall." Insisting that life is nothing more than a journey through an endless valley of sorrow is just as false as claiming that it is always rosy and bright.

It is this essential realism that is at the heart of the blues outlook. It calls for you to look at life as it is, to acknowledge both its positive and negative aspects with equal clarity, neither exaggerating hardship nor glossing over the depths of pleasure. At its most elemental, this outlook is a means of psychological survival, a means of coping with whatever situation you might encounter in life. The blues provide a kind of accepting, realistic ground where all aspects of life—from birth to death, from hopelessness to triumph—are all equally recognized. If you live under the mistaken notion that you will never experience pain, the day that this pain comes will be all the more shocking and disturbing. Likewise, concentrating upon doom will keep you from seeing what joy there is in the world.

Perhaps the best summation of the blues outlook comes in a song called "Life Is Like That," written by pianist Memphis Slim. It goes like this:

> *You got to cry a little, die a little,*
> *O life is like that,*
> *Well, that's what you've got to do,*
> *Well, and if you don't understand,*
> *People, I'm sorry for you.*
>
> *Sometimes you'll be held up, sometimes held down,*
> *Well, and sometimes your best friends don't even*
> *want you around. . . .*
>
> *There's some things you got to keep, some things you*
> *gotta repeat,*
> *People, happiness, well, is never complete, you*
> *know. . . .*
>
> *Sometimes you'll be helpless, sometimes you'll be*
> *restless,*
> *Well, keep on strugglin', so long as you're not*
> *breathless. . . .*[3]

In this song, Memphis Slim shows pity for those who cannot come to terms with the hardships of life, those who cannot be realistic, those who would rather flee from difficulty rather than "keep on strugglin'." This psychological stance taken by Memphis Slim no doubt rises out of the harsh social realities experienced by African-Americans: you will encounter racism, he says, you will encounter discrimination, you will experience unnecessary pain—but don't let this stop you. Instead, recognize this pain—and survive.

Ma Rainey has an even more direct way of putting this. It comes in a line from her song "Southern Blues."

> House catch on fire, and ain't no water 'round,
> If your house catch on fire, and ain't no water round,
> Throw your trunk out the window, buildin' burn on down. . .[4]

If your house is burning, Rainey reminds us, don't pretend the flames aren't real. Instead, jump out the window—and survive.

It would seem, in a way, that all of this is pretty simple stuff. Of course if your house is on fire, you're going to try to get out with your life. Of course life is both easy and difficult. It's surprising, though, how few art forms take this realistic approach: for the most part, art tries to present an idealized, unreal world. I've already mentioned how fabulously silly most television is, but this is also true for more well-respected art forms. Take the tradition of European portrait painting, for example. Rather than presenting an accurate picture of the sitting subject, it has long been understood, from the time of Da Vinci onward, that the painter should somehow *improve* the subject's looks, that the painter should somehow make the subject look more noble, more gentle, more gallant than he or she really is. The blues, at their most essential, do not do this. If the emperor is walking around without any clothes, the blues aren't afraid to say, "Man, he's naked."

It is this honesty, this insistence upon authenticity, that draws so many people to the blues outlook. ("You can't sing the blues unless you've had them," Leadbelly once said.) Looking for truth, listeners find it in the straightforward lyrics of Charley Patton, Leadbelly, and Muddy Waters.

Yet this authenticity should be taken in context. It must be remembered that the blues are, first and foremost, an art

A young, natty Big Bill Broonzy (1893–1958)

form. Blues musicians do not invent these sometimes chilling and sometimes liberating visions without a great deal of work, premeditation, and discipline. This message of truthtelling is achieved through the careful manipulation of words and music, by the accumulation of technique, by years of dedication, by mastering this form of art. The blues, for example, would not be nearly as effective if they were simply unadorned recitals of the pleasant and unpleasant facts of life. They are effective in proportion to the amount of artistry involved. The way a guitar player bends a string, the way a singer shouts in pain or joy: these are the means by which the blues succeed or fail. An inferior artist with a limited command of his or her craft, however honest and wellmeaning, will never capture the hearts and imagination of those who listen. Instead, such capture falls solely to the truthtellers who are also in absolute command of their work.

In short, the blues outlook is this: acknowledge the realities of life and triumph over them through the quality of your art.

A more personal example of this comes from Big Bill Broonzy, telling of his early life.

> I was born in Mississippi, in the year 18 and 93 [sic]. I was born on a plantation and I stayed there until I was eight years old. Then my daddy and mother, they brought us—me and my twin sister and about eight more of us—to Arkansas—that was Langdale—Langdale, Arkansas. . . . I was raised there. My daddy started a crop and I help chop cotton and pick cotton and my daddy said, "You can plow when you're fifteen."
>
> Every night I would bring me some cornstalks home and I'd go out in back of the barn and rub them cornstalks together and make music and the children would dance. That was my cornstalk fiddle. I rubbed it hard when I wanted a loud tone and I rubbed it easy when I wanted to play soft. . . .[5]

This passage is an apt allegory for the entire story of the blues. A young boy, in difficult circumstances, finds refuge in music, even if it is made from cornstalks. He learns to master these cornstalks: by playing them hard, by playing them soft, he discovers the capacities and qualities of his instrument. This same boy grows up and plays the blues around the world, taking him as far away from Langdale, Arkansas, as one could ever imagine. But more importantly, the music he turned to gave him strength, wisdom, and meaning.

No one could ask any more of art.

Heard the
Blues Today

And the blues today?

Throughout their history, ever since W. C. Handy recognized their power and originality as he sat waiting at that train station in Mississippi, the blues have, from time to time, been regarded as strangely mysterious, ghostly—even distant. There sometimes seems to be something fragile, and fading, about the blues, and so with each rise and fall of their popularity, someone invariably suggests that the blues are, sadly, "dying out."

No doubt this "mysterious" and "fragile" reputation has a great deal to do with the reality that the early history of the blues simply will never be known. There is an amount of uncertainty to the blues. Likewise, many of its most famous players led short, nomadic lives, leaving behind only a few inscrutable footprints, thus creating a blues pantheon of spectral, wandering figures. Finally, this air of mystery is increased by the fact that many blues historians and writers (like myself) come from a background far removed from, in Alan Lomax's phrase, "the land where the blues began." As a result, there is an obvious degree of distance to their work. Poring over lists of recording dates, interviewing musicians, piecing together story after story in an attempt to create a comprehensive whole, the blues can seem to be some kind of code that one must decipher, some strange and secret language known only by a few.

And hence always in danger of dying out.

There has been a lot of hand-wringing concerning the fate of the blues. Certainly public interest in them has varied widely over the years, and so it is understandable that those who care about the blues are sometimes in a state of near hysteria. The blues, they are afraid, will be forgotten. They will no longer be played. No one will remember the great names of Son House, Blind Lemon Jefferson, and Ma Rainey. The blues will finally, as has long been threatened, disappear into the mists of history. With such a grave prognosis, you can see why various musical doctors have been brought in from time to time to weigh in with profound pronouncements concerning the health of this patient called "the blues."

But there is no need to worry. Today more blues recordings are available than ever before. Almost every record store in the country has a section devoted entirely to the blues, and every year more and more blues music is being put out on CD—some of it becoming available for the first time. (For example, Robert Johnson's complete work was not released until 1990.) Across the country, various cities and towns hold festivals dedicated solely to the blues. Radio stations devote hours to tracing the careers of blues musicians. While it's true that the blues do not have the mass popularity of say, pop rock, blues records—like jazz records—have topped the charts in America. Even in the days of the blues's greatest popularity—the 1930s, 1960s, and 1990s—sales of blues records were nowhere the sales of recordings by mainstream performers. Yet like great literature or painting, the importance of the music does not lie in how many blues records have sold. The importance of the blues lies in their inherent artistic value, of which they have a great deal.

Another reason for feeling confident about the fate of the blues is that a number of great blues musicians are among us, working at the top of their forms. Along with John Lee Hooker, these men and women make up the current generation blues players.

B. B. King (1925—   ) and Lucille in 1969

Riley "B. B." King

Nobody loves me but my mother,
And she could be jivin' too. . . .
                    —B. B. King[1]

His playing takes him from Las Vegas to Amsterdam, from Chicago to Tokyo, and Riley "B. B." King continues to fill his constantly packed concert schedule, although age and diabetes have somewhat reduced his performance schedule (he did 342 shows in 1956). Born in 1925, King is old enough to have been exposed at any early age to some of the finest blues playing of all time, yet at the same time he has been able to add new dimensions to the music over the years through his own innovations. Graceful, kindhearted, and inspired, King has forever left his mark upon the blues.

Raised in poverty in Indianola, Mississippi, the son of sharecroppers, Riley King gained the nickname B. B. while working in 1949 as a disc jockey for station WDIA in Memphis, Tennessee. At the time, King's on-air handle was The Beale Street Blues Boy, but his listeners soon shortened it to B. B. Regardless of what he was called, King had other destinations than the radio station in mind. He was determined to become a professional blues musician, and one classic story reveals King's intense commitment to this goal.

About the same time he became a full-time disc jockey, King was playing guitar in a small dance hall in Twist, Arkansas. In the course of the evening, two men got into a fight over a woman who today is known only as Lucille. Words and threats soon developed into punches, and as the two men sparred on the dance hall floor, one of them knocked over a kerosene heater. In a matter of moments, the hall was on fire. Everyone who could rushed outside—some weren't so lucky, the blaze claimed two lives—but once he was outside King realized that he'd left his guitar onstage. Without thinking, he bolted back into the burning building and emerged unharmed, clutching his precious guitar. Only then, shaking his head in wonder, did he realize the recklessness of his act. In honor of the moment, and the woman who'd inspired the goings on, King dubbed his guitar "Lucille"—and has kept the name ever since.

Not long after this incident, King was able to leave radio behind. He recorded a hit song, "Three o'Clock Blues"—which in 1951 reached number one on the rhythm-and-blues charts and stayed there for seventeen weeks—and his career was launched. Soon, King was fronting his own band at such notable venues as the Apollo Theater in New York City.

Almost from the outset of his career, King was interested in working in a band format rather than appearing solo. And not just any band: King was vastly impressed with such performers as Count Basie and Duke Ellington, whose large, orchestral bands were able to produce the big, multidimensional sound that King wanted for his own music. As early as 1955, King was touring with a twelve-piece band, complete with horns and backup singers, which was a distinctly original departure from most blues players. Unlike most of his contemporaries, King was intrigued by the complexities of sounds and shadings that were possible with a larger group of musicians. Diverging from the aggressive roar of Muddy Waters's guitar playing, King shaped his own more delicate, seamless, and shapely style. His resulting guitar solos—such as those featured on the 1965 recording, *Live at the Regal*, which is one of the greatest blues works of all time—reach the level of artistry formerly demonstrated only by Louis Armstrong and his trumpet. In recognition of the sophistication of his work, King was awarded an honorary doctorate in music by Yale University.

In 1970, King scored another enormous hit with his version of "The Thrill Is Gone." This song—written by Roy Hawkins but enhanced immeasurably by King's consummate singing and guitar playing—is one of the most widely known of all blues compositions. And as if this wasn't enough for a single career, King has gone on recording and touring: in 1988 the Irish rock band U2 included and honored King on their album *Rattle and Hum*, and King continues to play in cities across the country. When he reaches your part of town, be sure and see him. No one alive plays the blues any better than King.

On a less monumental level, King also runs a tasty restaurant and well-frequented blues club on Beale Street in Memphis. Highly recommended is the barbecue lunch plate— and any Saturday night.

Etta James

The tradition of Ma Rainey and Bessie Smith lives on in the form of Etta James. Just as these two legendary singers did, James expresses a kaleidoscope of emotion. Ample and explosive, her warm voice is an instrument of seemingly endless potential. She can be explosively bawdy on such songs as "Good Rockin' Daddy," or openly heartrending with a blues song like "I'd Rather Go Blind." Humor, rage, celebration, sorrow, James does it all. As with the best of blues

Etta James (1938–   ) poses for an early publicity shot.

performers, listening to her you get the impression that she isn't just singing about things she's read in a book, seen on television, or heard through the grapevine. She's talking about life as she has lived it. Authenticity of emotion in combination with exquisite artisty gives James her enormous power and appeal.

Born in Los Angeles in 1938, James and her family moved soon after to San Francisco.[2] Her earliest exposure to music came through the church, where she learned to sing in the choir. By the time she was a teenager she was already interested in rhythm and blues. Throughout the following years, James had a number of hits on the rhythm-and-blues charts, including "The Wallflower" (1954), "All I Could Do Was Cry" (1960), "Something's Got a Hold of Me" (1961), "Stop the Wedding" (1962), "Pushover" (1963), and "Tell Mama" (1968). While these songs remain entertaining, they are essentially formulaic rhythm and blues, similar in style and content to the work of other singers. They don't reveal the true depths of emotion that James was capable of reaching. In contrast to Billie Holiday, whose best work was done at the very beginning of her career, James would have to wait, suffer some hard knocks, and then work her way back into the music scene before she would reveal the full range of her talent.

By 1971, despite her track record of hits, James found herself without a recording contract. The 1970s were a bad time for the blues, and James was not immune to the downward turn. By this time, she had been a professional performer for almost twenty years, but none of that seemed to matter: since she did not sing disco or funk, record executives, club owners, and tour promoters thought her music was "old-fashioned." One can only imagine how frustrating it must have been to know that she possessed all the skills one could hope for in a singer, yet she could find few opportunities to display her vast ability.

Nevertheless, she persevered. She began playing one-night stands in small clubs and bars (every one a long way down from the larger halls she'd previously commanded). Living on what she could earn from week to week, James stayed in run-down hotels, drank coffee in all-night restaurants, and resolved to establish herself once again as an outstanding and recognized performer. Slowly her diligence began to pay off. Her reputation as a powerful singer began to grow again, by word of mouth, by a succession of favorable reviews, and by the increasing respect felt toward her by other musicians. By 1978, James had truly returned. It was then that she opened for the Rolling Stones, exposing herself to the largest audiences she had ever known.

She has not looked back since. She is still performing, still recording, her power undiminished.

Ironically, her exile from the music scene may have contributed to her strength and range of expression. Perhaps reflecting the hurt she must have felt at this time, the music she has recorded since her return is richer, more personal, more heartfelt, and more adventurous than that which she did in the 1950s and 1960s. This newfound mastery might be due to her simple maturation as a musician, but that's doubtful. The difference between the music in her earlier and later periods is too profound: Etta James learned something about herself while she was out on the road, when it seemed that no one wanted to hear her, when she had the blues. The core of pride and strength that she found is now evident in all her music. She is a survivor.

Buddy Guy

Another survivor is the guitar virtuoso Buddy Guy. Among blues musicians, Guy is undoubtedly one of the most influential, and yet strangely overlooked, guitarists of all time. Other, more famous players, such as Eric Clapton, Jeff Beck, and the late Stevie Ray Vaughan and Jimi Hendrix, have all paid homage to Guy, admitting how much his playing meant to them. At their one meeting, Hendrix even told Guy that he canceled a show in order to meet the man from whom he had stolen "a lot of licks." Nevertheless, Guy has rarely received much acclaim, and it has only been in the past few years, following the release of two Grammy-winning albums, *Damn Right I've Got the Blues,* and *Feels Like Rain,* that he finally got the attention he deserves.[3]

Now in his late fifties and still going strong, Guy was born the son of cotton farmers in Lettsworth, Louisiana. Self-taught, Guy knew as a boy that he wanted to play the blues, and yet he was also afflicted with such a profound and crippling shyness that he was not sure if he could ever become a professional musician. As Guy tells it,

> On a rainy day, I would lie in front of the radio and fall asleep listening to Muddy Waters or Howlin' Wolf. I would dream that was me. All these people would be looking at me, and I was standing there playing. And I wasn't shy. I'd wake up and say, "Wow, that was me." Then I'd stop and say, "No, that wasn't close. You can't do that in front of nobody."[4]

Fighting this shyness and self-doubt every day, Guy moved from Louisiana to Chicago in 1957, in hopes of making a living at playing the blues. His guitar playing was already so extraordinary that none other than Muddy Waters, Guy's radio idol, took him under his wing and asked him to play second guitar on his upcoming album. This was to be Waters's classic *Folk Singer.* But even this prestigious gig did not cure Guy of his unreasonable shyness and self-doubt concerning his guitar playing. Waters at one point even got so frustrated with Guy's endless worrying about his ability that Muddy literally slapped Guy in the face, saying, "I don't want to hear that from you. You gonna play."[5] This might seem like pretty harsh treatment, but according to Guy it was exactly this kind of shock that he needed to get him past his fear of failure.

Perhaps to compensate for the fact that he was otherwise so painfully shy, Guy developed a maniacal, pyrotechnic style of playing. Long before Hendrix made it popular and supposedly revolutionized guitar playing, Guy was already using feedback from his amplifier to create stunning

*Buddy Guy (1937–), left, and Otis Rush (1934–)
in 1994. Many blues and rock musicians have
imitated Guy's driving guitar style.*

psychedelic effects. Likewise, many of Hendrix's stage tricks—playing the guitar on his knees, playing behind his back, and so on—were taken directly from Guy. Despite his obvious, flamboyant skill, however, it took Guy almost another ten years to finally summon up the confidence to strike out on his own as the leader of a band. It was while he was doing this, during a tour of England in 1965, that a young Eric Clapton saw Guy playing live at a place called the Marquee Club. He was the first amplified bluesman Clapton had ever seen, and, in a sense, Guy was passing on the torch that had been handed to him by Muddy Waters.

In all likelihood it was Guy's age and his unique place in the generations of blues musicians, that contributed to the fact that he was commercially overlooked for so long. By the time Guy was striking out on his own, the relatively small blues market was already taken up by the established older generation of Muddy Waters, Howlin' Wolf, and John Lee Hooker. Then, ironically, it was the younger generation behind him—the very players he influenced—who seized the spotlight. To most record company executives in the late 1960s, Buddy Guy sounded as if he was simply imitating Eric Clapton and Jimi Hendrix, when, in fact, *they* had imitated *him*.

Guy never grew bitter about this lack of attention. Guy is a tremendously kind and generous man: generous enough that he didn't begrudge the success of these younger musicians. Instead, he simply continued to play the music he loved, going without a recording contract for twelve-and-a-half years, drawing so much inspiration from the blues that he "even forgot what down is like. Even when I'm down, I think I'm up."[6] Guy has also helped out countless other blues musicians by managing Legends, a well-known Chicago blues club. By offering new musicians a place to play, Guy has helped nurture and guide the next blues generation.

Guy has said about his playing, "If I'm going to do it, I want to do it to death." With this kind of persistence, Guy has finally begun to receive his due.

Robert Cray

Along with Stevie Ray Vaughan, the Texas guitarist who met his untimely death in a 1990 helicopter crash, no one has contributed more to today's surging popularity of the blues than Robert Cray. Cray's guitar playing is subtle, soulful, and quietly stunning. And because he produces an innovative blend of blues, soul, gospel, and pop—without reducing the power of any of them—he has exposed his music to more people than any other current-generation blues musician. For example, his landmark 1986 album *Strong Persuader* has sold more than a million copies, virtually unheard of for a blues work.

Originally from Columbus, Georgia, Cray and his family settled in Tacoma, Washington, when he was fifteen.[7] First trained on the piano, Cray later learned to play the guitar—perhaps influenced by Jimi Hendrix, a Seattle native whose shadow looms large over many musicians from the Pacific Northwest.[8] In 1969, the young Cray met guitarist Albert Collins and through him found his true vocation: the blues. After this, Cray formed his own blues band and built up a strong local following.

Incorporating other influences such as the soul sound of Sam Cooke and Ray Charles, Cray and his band began releasing a series of albums that would eventually establish him as one of the leading bluesmen of his generation. His first three efforts—*Who's Been Talkin'*, *Bad Influence*, and *False Accusations*—gave ample evidence of his talent, but sales were flat. His fourth and fifth albums, however, changed everything. *Showdown!* won Cray a Grammy, sold a quarter of a million copies, and paved the way for the epic *Strong Persuader*, which won yet another Grammy. The video Cray made for "Smoking Gun," the hit off this album, was perhaps the first all-blues video ever played on MTV's heavy rotation—a remarkable achievement considering that at this time MTV rarely departed from its standard formula of featuring young, white rock bands. (Since then, with features such as *Yo! MTV Raps*, the video giant has obviously loosened up considerably—or, to take a more cynical view, it has at last recognized the marketability of African-American music.) Cray's music, however, was so strong that it did not recognize these kinds of corporate boundaries: he was simply too good, his appeal simply too plain.

Since then, Cray has won a third Grammy for *Don't Be Afraid of the Dark*; toured the United States, Canada, Europe, and Asia; and has played with other legendary musicians such as Keith Richard and Eric Clapton. Presently in mid-career, it is impossible to say how much more Cray will accomplish, but he is already a part of blues history.

The list of performers who deserve attention goes on: Johnny Copeland, Joanna Connor, Charlie Musselwhite, Taj Mahal, Bobby Radcliffe, Marva White, Jimmy Witherspoon, and Mitch Woods. They continue to work solidly within the blues tradition, and are consummate musicians. In a sense, I'd have preferred to concentrate on these and other lesser-known players: the blues, after all, are first about everyday struggle, about our common fates, and about the strength to go on in the face of sometimes desperate odds. Once you get into the airy realms of fame, million-dollar deals, and world tours, your perspective on the whole thing starts to go, and it becomes easy to forget that the blues have always risen out of hard work, dedication, and patience. Even the most famous blues players will tell that success didn't happen overnight, it never came easy, and there were times when they coubted their own worth and ability. The key remains in keeping on.

There are other ways in which the blues live on, besides in those musicians who continue to play them. In strictly musical terms, the blues are the basis for the genres of rock, rap, soul, and jazz—and in that sense, as long as these forms of music survive, so will the blues. But perhaps more importantly, the blues philosophy and outlook continues to inspire countless artists.

Take Bruce Springsteen, for example. In many of his songs—often influenced by Woody Guthrie, who in turn was influenced by Leadbelly—Springsteen adopts the same realistic attitude that informs so many blues compositions. Life can be hard, Springsteen says, so you've got to work to survive. Or as

Arrested Development delivers at a live performance.

the words from his song "Thunder Road" put it, "it's a town for losers, and I'm pullin' out of here to win." Springsteen's most recent hit, "Philadelphia," is in its spirit essentially a blues song: one about living with AIDS. Springsteen's mournful vocals on this song are in a direct line descending from Charley Patton, Son House, and the numberless other blues singers who have been forgotten with the passage of time, but whose style of articulating pain has not.

The members of the rap group Arrested Development share a similar musical vision. Their song "Everyday People," for example, expresses the same truth-telling, unromanticized attitude toward life that Bessie Smith gave us—while their song "Revolution," from the *Malcolm X* soundtrack, speaks to the same desire and demand for justice that has always been a part of the blues. Thus, in both style and content, the blues continue to thrive.

In reading this book, you may have picked up on some of the spirit as well. No other art form has taught me more about life—how to live and appreciate it—than the blues. They are, for me, essential wisdom: a code of meaning,

143

conduct, and insight. Whether they will become these same things for you, I don't know. That will depend upon whether this book, for you, is an end in itself or merely an introduction. I could wish no one a more generous fate than to become steeped in the lore, traditions, and truth of the blues.

Source Notes

One

1. Robert Palmer, *Deep Blues* (New York: Penguin Books, 1981), p. 45. Other descriptions of Handy's first exposure to the blues can be found in *The Land Where the Blues Began* by Alan Lomax (New York: Pantheon Books, 1993) and Handy's autobiography, *Father of the Blues (An Autobiography)*, (New York: Da Capo, 1990).
2. Sandra Lieb, *Mother of the Blues: A Study of Ma Rainey* (Amherst: University of Massachusetts Press, 1981), p. 3.
3. Lawrence Cohn, ed., *Nothing But the Blues* (New York: Abbeville Press, 1993), p. 18.
4. Ibid., p. 14.
5. Frederick Douglass, *My Bondage and My Freedom* (New York: Miller, Orton & Mulligan, 1855), p. 97.
6. William Barlow, *Looking up at Down: The Emergence of Blues Culture* (Philadelphia: Temple University Press, 1989), p. 18.
7. Paul Oliver, Max Harrison, and William Bolcom, *The New Grove Gospel, Blues and Jazz* (New York: W. W. Norton, 1986), p. 21.
8. Barlow, p. 10.

Two

1. Cohn, ed., p. 45.
2. The principal source for the information presented on Blind Lemon Jefferson comes from the section on him in Sam Charters, *The Country Blues* (New York: Da Capo, 1975).
3. Peter Guralnick, *Searching for Robert Johnson* (New York: Dutton, 1989), p. 26.
4. *The Complete Recordings of Robert Johnson,* (CBS 467246 2), liner notes and transcriptions by Steve LaVere.

Three

1. James Lincoln Collier, *The Making of Jazz (A Comprehensive History)* (New York: Dell Publishing, 1978), p. 142.
2. Lieb, above, and Barlow, above, are the principal sources for information presented on Ma Rainey.
3. Barlow, pp. 170-71.
4. Ibid., pp. 172-73.

Five

1. Charles Wolfe and Kip Lornell, *The Life and Legend of Leadbelly* (New York: HarperCollins, 1992), p. 254. This is the principal source for information presented on Leadbelly.
2. Albert Murray, *Stomping the Blues*, (New York: Vintage, 1982), p. 126. It is important to note that this is not necessarily Murray's own assessment of Holiday: it is his succinct summation of certain attitudes toward her.
3. In his book *Billie's Blues* (New York: Stein and Day, 1978), James Chilton has done an excellent job in sorting through the facts and fantasies of Billie Holiday's life. His is the principal source for information presented on Holiday.
4. Palmer, p. 5.
5. Ibid., p. 12.
6. Ibid., p. 260.

Six

1. Alan Lomax, *Land Where the Blues Began* (New York: Pantheon Books, 1993), p. 406.
2. Bob Brunning, *Blues: The British Connection* (New York: Poole, 1986), p. 10.
3. Philip Norman, *Symphony for the Devil: The Rolling Stones Story* (New York: Linden Press/Simon & Schuster, 1984), p. 68.
4. Ibid, p. 44.
5. Marc Roberty, *Slowhand: The Life and Music of Eric Clapton* (New York: Crown Trade Paperbacks, 1993), p. 11.
6. Principal sources for information presented on Lightnin' Hopkins are Sam Charters's *The Country Blues and The Legacy of the Blues (Art and Lives of Twelve Great Bluesmen)* (New York: Da Capo, 1977).
7. The principal source for information presented on John Lee Hooker is Robert Santelli's *Big Book of the Blues* (New York: Penguin, 1993), pp. 184-86.

Seven

1. Ralph Ellison, *Shadow and Act*, 1953. 1964. (New York: Vintage, 1972), p. 78
2. Ellison, p. 140
3. Memphis Slim, Big Bill Broonzy, and Sonny Boy Williamson, *Blues in the Mississippi Night* (Salem, Massachusetts: Rykodisc CRCD 90155), 1990. As told to and recorded by Alan Lomax. Notes and transcription by Alan Lomax.
4. Lieb, p. 159.
5. Lomax, pp. 426-27.

Eight

1. Charles Sawyer, *The Arrival of B. B. King* (New York: Da Capo, 1980), p. 147.

2. Santelli, p. 206.
3. Ed Enright, "Buddy Guy: Sweet Home Success," *Down Beat*, February 1995, p. 17.
4. Donald E. Wilcock with Buddy Guy. *Damn Right I've Got the Blues: Buddy Guy and the Blues Roots of Rock-and-Roll*, (San Francisco: Woodford Press, 1993), p. 16.
5. Jas Obrecht, ed. *Blues Guitar: The Men Who Made the Music*, (San Francisco: GPI Books, 1990), p. 143.
6. Santelli, p. 206.
7. *Ibid.*, p. 106.
8. "Hear My Train A-Comin," from Hendrix's *Live at Winterland*, is a classic blues performance.

Recommended Reading

These books, as well as those included in the preceding notes, are good reading for anyone interested in the blues.

Baker, Houston A. *Blues, Ideology, and Afro-American Literature*. Chicago: University of Chicago Press, 1984.

Charters, Samuel B. *The Bluesmakers*. New York: Da Capo, 1991.

_____ . *The Roots of the Blues (An African Search)*. New York: Da Capo, 1991.

Cone, James. *The Spirituals and the Blues: An Interpretation*. New York: Seabury Press, 1972.

Dahl, Linda. *Stormy Weather (The Music and Lives of Century of Jazzwomen)*. New York: Limelight Editions, 1989.

Epstein, Dana. *Sinful Tunes and Spirituals: Black Folk Music to the Civil War*. Urbana: University of Illinois Press, 1977.

Evans, David. *Big Road Blues (Tradition and Creativity in the Folk Blues)*. New York: Da Capo, 1982.

Garon, Paul. *Blues and the Poetic Spirit*. New York: Da Capo, 1978.

Genovese, Eugene D. Roll, Jordan, *Roll: The World the Slaves Made*. New York: Pantheon Book, 1974.

Harrison, Daphne Duvall. *Black Pearls: Blues Queens of the 1920s*. New Brunswick: Rutgers University Press, 1988.

Herzhaft, Gerard. *Encyclopedia of the Blues*. Fayetteville: University of Arkansas Press, 1992.

Jones, LeRoi. *Blues People*. New York: Apollo Editions, 1963.

Leman, Nicholas. *The Promised Land (The Great Black Migration and How It Changed America)*. New York: Vintage, 1991.

McKee, Margaret, and Fred Chisenhall. *Beale Black and Blue: Life and Music on Black America's Main Street*. Baton Rouge: Louisiana State University Press, 1981.

Oliver, Paul. *Blues Fell This Morning (Meaning in the Blues)*. Cambridge: Cambridge University Press, 1990.

Sackheim, Eric, ed. *The Blues Line: A Collection of Blues Lyrics*. New York: Ecco Press, 1993.

Recommended Listening

The following is not meant to represent an exhaustive overview of the blues. It is meant to illustrate the work of the artists mentioned here and to give a suggestion of the wealth of recorded blues. The selections can be obtained through almost any record store and which is often available at larger public libraries. Like this book, the list is only a place to begin and reflects my own biases.

Louis Armstrong
> *Louis Armstrong—the Hot Fives, Vol. I*/Columbia (CK 44049)
> *Louis Armstrong—the Hot Fives and Hot Sevens, Vol. II*/Columbia (CK 44253)
> *Louis Armstrong—the Hot Fives and Hot Sevens, Vol. III*/Columbia (CK 44422)
> *Louis Armstrong of New Orleans*/MCA (MCAD-42328)

Big Bill Broonzy
> *Big Bill Broonzy Sings Folk Songs*/Smithsonian Folkways (CD SF 40023)
Big Bill Broonzy, 1934–1947/Story of the Blues (3504)
Robert Cray
> *Strong Persuader*/Mercury (830 568-1)

Reverend Gary Davis
> *Harlem Street Singer*/Prestige/Bluesville (OBCCD-547-2)

W. C. Handy
> *W. C. Handy: Father of the Blues*/DRG Records (SL 5192)

Jimi Hendrix
> *Live at Winterland*/Rykodisc (RCD 20038)

Billie Holiday
> *The Legacy (1933–1958)*/Columbia/Legacy
> *Lady in Autumn: The Best of the Verve Years*/Verve
> *The Billie Holiday Songbook*/Verve

John Lee Hooker
> *The Ultimate Collection: 1948–1990*/Rhino (R2-70572)
> *John Lee Hooker Plays & Sings the Blues*/Chess (MCA) (CHD 9199)
> *The Healer*/Chameleon (74808-2)
> *The Real Folk Blues*/MCA-Chess (CHD 9271)
> *The Best of John Lee Hooker*/MCA-Chess (MCAD 10539)

Lightnin' Hopkins
> *The Complete Prestige/Bluesville Recordings*/Prestige/ Bluesville (7PCD 4406-2)
> *The Complete Alladin Recordings*/EMI (CDP 7-96843-2)
> *Double Blues*/Fantasy (FCD 24702-2)
> *Lightnin' Hopkins*/Smithsonian/Folkways (CD SF40019)

Son House
> *Delta Blues: The Original Library of Congress Sessions from Field Recordings, 1941–1942*/Biograph (BCD 118 ADD)
> *Father of the Delta Blues: The Complete 1965 Sessions*/ Columbia (48867)

Death Letter/Edsel (EDCD 167)

Howlin' Wolf
Howlin' Wolf (box set)/MCA-Chess (CHC3-9332)
The Real Folk Blues/MCA-Chess (9273)
More Real Folk Blues/MCA-Chess (9279)

Mississippi John Hurt
The Best of Mississippi John Hurt/Vanguard (VCD 19/20)

Etta James
Etta James Live/Rhino (R271742)
Etta James Rocks the House/MCA-Chess (CH 9184)
Her Greatest Sides, Vol. 1/MCA-Chess (CH 9110)

Blind Lemon Jefferson
King of the Country Blues/Blind Lemon Jefferson/Yazoo
(1069)

Blind Willie Johnson
The Complete Blind Willie Johnson/Columbia (C2K
52835)

Lonnie Johnson
Blues by Lonnie Johnson/Original Blues Classics (502)
Lonnie Johnson, 1926–1940/Blues Documents (2064)
The Complete Folkways Recordings/Smithsonian-
Folkways (SF 40067)

Robert Johnson
The Complete Recordings of Robert Johnson/Columbia
(C2K 46222)

B. B. King
King of the Blues (box set)/MCA (D4-10677)
The Best of B. B. King, Vol. 1/Flair (Virgin) (86230)
Live at the Regal/Mobile Fidelity Sound Labs (UDCD 01-
00548)

Leadbelly
  King of the 12-String Guitar/Columbia (CK 46776)
  Alabama Bound/RCA (9600-2)
  Leadbelly Sings Folk Songs/Smithsonian-Folkways (SF 40010)

Blind Willie McTell
  Blind Willie McTell (1927-1935)/Yazoo (1037)
  Complete Library of Congress Recordings/RST (BDCD 6001)
  Blind Willie McTell, Last Sessions/Yazoo (1041)

Memphis Minnie
  Memphis Minnie, Vol. 1/Blues Classics (1)
  Memphis Minnie, Vol. 2/Blues Classics (13)

Memphis Slim
  Life Is Like That/Charly (CD 249)
  Memphis Slim: The Real Folk Blues/Chess (9250)

Charley Patton
  Founder of the Delta Blues/Yazoo (1020)
  King of the Delta Blues/Yazoo (2001)
  Charley Patton: The Complete Recorded Works/Pea Vine (PCD 2255/6/7)

Ma Rainey
  Ma Rainey's Black Bottom/Yazoo (1071)
  The Immortal Ma Rainey/Milestone (2001)

Jimmy Rushing
  The Essential Jimmy Rushing/Vanguard (65-66)

Bessie Smith
  The Complete Recordings of Bessie Smith, Vol. 1/Columbia (C2K 47091)
  The Complete Recordings of Bessie Smith, Vol. 2/Columbia (C2K 47471)

The Complete Recordings of Bessie Smith, Vol.3/
Columbia (C2K 47474)
*The Complete Recordings of Bessie Smith, Vol. 4/*Columbia (C2K 52838)
*Bessie Smith, The Collection/*Columbia (C2K 52768)

Roosevelt Sykes
*The Country Blues Piano Ace/*Yazoo (1033)
*The Honeydripper, 1929–1941/*Blues Documents (2013)
*The Honeydripper, Vol. 2., 1936–1951/*Blues Documents (2088)

Sonny Terry
*Sonny's Story/*Original Blues Classics (OBC 503)
*Sonny Is King/*Original Blues Classics (OBC 521)
*The Folkways Years, 1941-1963/*Smithsonian-Folkways (SF 40033)

Big Joe Turner
*Greatest Hits/*Atlantic (81752)

Stevie Ray Vaughan
*Texas Flood/*Epic (EK 38734)
*Couldn't Stand the Weather/*Epic (EK 39304)

Mose Vinson
Mystery Train (with Junior Parker, James Cotton, Pat Hare/Rounder (CD SS 38)

Dinah Washington
*Dinah Washington Sings the Blues/*Mercury (832 573-2)
*First Issue: The Dinah Washington Story/*Mercury-Verve (514841)

Muddy Waters
*Muddy Waters: The Chess Box/*MCA-Chess (31268)
*The Best of Muddy Waters/*MCA-Chess (31268)

Muddy Waters at Newport/MCA-Chess (31269)
The Real Folk Blues/MCA-Chess (9274)
More Real Folk Blues/MCA-Chess (9278)
They Call Me Muddy Waters/MCA-Chess (9299)
Hard Again/CBS (PZ 34449)

Index

45, 56

Thoroughgood, George, 120

"Toby Time." *See* Theater Owners Booking Association

"Twelve-bar blues," 65

Urban blues. *See* City blues

Vaudeville, 12, 45, 50, 51, 71

Vaughan, Stevie Ray, 137, 141

Walker, Frank, 56

Waters, Muddy. *See* Muddy Waters

Watts, Issac, 18

Winters, Johnny, 94

Work songs, 15–17, 25